The Handbook of Performance Management

About the Editor

Frances Neale has been an editor and journalist for over 20 years, specialising in human resource management. A former manager at IPM and editor of *IPM Digest*, she has worked on books and reports for organisations as diverse as UNESCO (in Paris), ORC Inc (in New York) and British publishers Morgan Grampian, McGraw-Hill, Kogan Page and Pergamon. Also a professionally qualified photographer, she carries out both photographic and editorial assignments for various organisations, including the Manpower Society and Satterfield Satellite Enterprises.

The Handbook of Performance Management

Edited by Frances Neale

Institute of Personnel Management

First published in 1991
Reprinted 1993

© Institute of Personnel Management 1991

Phototypeset by Intype, London
and printed in Great Britain by
Short Run Press Ltd, Exeter

British Library Cataloguing in Publication Data
The handbook of performance management.
  I. Neale, Frances
  658.314
ISBN 0–85292–469–0

Paperback edn 0 85292 483 6

Contents

About the Contributors

Tricia Allison is a pioneer of stress counselling in the workplace. After completing her postgraduate professional training in 1971, she gained wide experience in counselling, training and management. More recently, she set up the first in-house professional counselling service within the TSB, now adopted at national level. From 1986 until early 1991 she introduced and ran a stress counselling service in The Post Office, working with the University of Manchester on the first independently evaluated project on stress counselling in organisations. She is now an independent counsellor and employee counselling consultant. She has contributed to a number of TV documentaries and to publications on workplace stress counselling and on criminal assault at work.

Roger Holdsworth, MA, is a psychology graduate of Cambridge University whose early professional experience in psychometric assessment and staff development was with a pioneering Swedish consultancy. He then joined the National Institute of Industrial Psychology in London, where he became head of training, responsible for NIIP test development and supply, and for vocational guidance. For five years he practised as an independent consultant in assessment and training projects such as the IPM/NCC co-ordinated research project with Nottingham University, examining the use and validity of psychometric testing in graduate selection. In 1977 he founded Saville and Holdsworth Ltd with Peter Saville, where he has been involved in a wide range of assessment projects, including courses in assessment centres, interviewing methods and personality measurement, and in developing occupational tests and Occupational Personality Questionnaires. Currently Managing Director of SHL Europe in Paris, his publications include *Personnel Selection Testing – a Guide for Managers*, *Identifying Managerial Potential* and (with Ruth Lancashire) *Career Change*.

Alan Mumford, DLitt, CIPM, has extensive experience in management development, holding posts with John Laing and Sons, IPC Magazines and ICL, as well as a spell as a Deputy Chief Training Adviser at the Department of Employment and six years as Executive Resources Adviser to the Chloride Group. In 1983 he was appointed Professor of Management Development at International Management Centres, where he was responsible for developing their approach to improving management performance through effective learning processes. He has also worked with senior managers and directors in a variety of organisations including Ford of Europe, Pilkington and Swan Hunter. He now works part-time for IMC while running his own consultancy. An active member of IPM, holding the office of Vice-President (Training and Development) in 1971–3, he has written or co-authored (often with Peter Honey) numerous articles and books on management development, including *The Manual of Learning Styles*, *The Manual of Learning Opportunities*, *Developing Top Managers* and, for IPM, *Management Development: Strategies for Action*.

Pam Pocock, MSc, is a graduate of the London Business School and former editor of the IPM journal, *Personnel Management*. She has wide consultancy experience in marketing and communications and has helped many organisations from major public companies to small start-up ventures. She was the Editorial Director of a large publishing company and most recently worked for Courtaulds as head of internal communication and corporate identity. As a Director of Strategic People she specialises in the management of change, organisational culture and business ethics and is responsible for the consultancy's training, development and communications work. She also conceived the business simulation, Dilemma!

Peter Wallum, BSc(Eng), ASRM, MIPM, is a Director of the consultancy Strategic People. From a background in engineering and occupational psychology, his early career included periods as a consultant in the international mining industry and Senior Manpower Planning Adviser to the Air Transport and Travel Industry Training Board. Other personnel posts include British Steel, where he was responsible for graduate recruitment and training, and Charterhouse, where he was both head of personnel and consultant to the many companies in which the group had an interest. Before establishing Strategic People, he was Personnel Director of Thomson Holidays. His main areas of interest are manpower and succession planning, management development and reward strategy. He has also worked internationally with financial services organisations.

Carol Whitaker, FIPM, is Head of Personnel with Black Horse Financial Services where she is responsible for personnel, training and development for over 1,500 staff. Recent initiatives have included appraisal training, cross-functional work groups and the introduction of job evaluation. In a career embracing most aspects of personnel management, she has held posts with House of Fraser, A C Nielson, Rank Radio International, the Meat and Livestock Commission, British Transport Docks Board and Harrods.

Stephen Williams has been Director of Human Resource Development with ICL since 1988, where he is responsible for HRD strategy and policy for over 20,000 employees, and has created and implemented the Investing in People programme. A graduate of Hull University, he previously held senior personnel posts with STC Telecommunications, P and O, and the Ford Motor Company.

Vicky Wright is a Director of Hay Management Consultants and heads their UK compensation and benefits practice. She has 18 years' experience in the personnel field, the majority spent in personnel management roles in both the private and public sectors. She has also spent a short time as Personnel Policy Adviser to the CBI. Her five years in HR management consultancy have involved her in assignments in the UK and abroad, mainly advising on compensation and benefits, culture change and organisation. A member of IPM, where she serves on the National Committee for Organisation and Human Resource Planning, she is a BSc of Durham University and a MSc of the London Business School.

The Performance Management Model

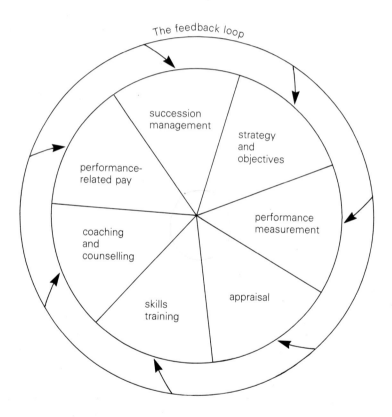

The feedback loop

succession management

strategy and objectives

performance-related pay

performance measurement

coaching and counselling

appraisal

skills training

Introduction

by Pamela Pocock

The early summer of 1991 will be remembered here in the UK as one of the coldest and wettest on record. (Things later picked up.) But it is not just the weather that we shall remember; there was also a deep recession which produced high levels of unemployment among the professional and managerial classes. However, these redundancies are not simply caused by the recession; there is something afoot in organisations. Many have been spurred on by management gurus such as Tom Peters, who wrote in his book *Thriving on Chaos:*[1]

> Structure kills. Most are moving to reduce it. Few are moving fast enough. Excess middle management staff – often to the tune of several hundred percent – still exists in most big firms and even in many smaller and mid-sized firms.
> No more than five layers of management are necessary, regardless of firm size; limit layers in any facility to three at most.

Chief executives have taken the message to heart and removed layers of managers from their organisations. As a result, the expectations from those who remain are exceedingly high. In *The Age of Unreason,*[2] Charles Handy has introduced us to the idea that there will only be a core of workers who are employed full time by organisations in the future. The rest of the workforce will have far more flexible relationships with the employer. Handy suggests that by the turn of the century only half of those with paid work will be in full-time employment, a reduction of 26% on current levels. Increasingly, therefore, organisations are under pressure to get the most out of their resources; recession puts the spotlight on cost control.

So, when the Institute of Personnel Management suggested a book on performance management, it could hardly have seemed more timely. Its most important feature, however, is that the contributions do not interpret performance management in a narrow fashion. Too many organisations associate the term exclusively with either their appraisal system or performance-related pay. Neither is appropriate, although both topics are, of course, covered within this book.

The approach has been to construe performance management in an holistic sense; the contents of the book are firmly set within the context of business planning and strategy. Individual objectives are dealt with as part of the objectives of the organisation as a whole. Managers are encouraged to coach, counsel and train people to improve their performance. Appraisal is seen as a continuing, year-round dialogue, and pay is recognised as only part of the process. Fortunately, the editor and authors of this book have recognised that these facets of performance management are not sufficient in themselves and that the outcomes must be built back into the business planning process. So, unusually, you will find here a chapter on succession management and a final word on how all the information must be fed back continually into business strategy.

The whole process is not simple and should probably be avoided by the faint-hearted. But the opportunities are great; good performance management provides a self-improving system for both individuals and the organisation. And when a company can demonstrate that it is truly listening to the needs of its employees, the benefits will always be seen in the bottom line.

As I have said earlier, performance management is often confused with performance-related pay. PRP is highly fashionable at the time of writing, with organisations throwing themselves into new pay schemes confident that they will solve all ills. In truth, PRP is as unlikely to work in the longer term as the management initiatives that preceded it. It is simply the most recent in a roll-call that might include management by objectives, total quality management, zero-based budgeting, matrix management, quality circles, team briefings and so on. All such initiatives are pointless unless they become part of the culture of the organisation.

If an organisation wishes to address issues of performance management, then performance must become one of the values of that organisation and the managers must be seen to live that value in their everyday lives. Hewlett Packard, for example, is an organisation which is well known for its values statement, the HP Way, which focuses on both attitudes to people and expectations of performance. Managers in HP understand the corporate philosophy and it guides their everyday activities.

So, if performance is important to an organisation, which in today's climate it surely must be, then there is a need for it to become a deep-rooted part of the culture. For this to happen, there needs to be a well thought out performance management system working throughout the organisation.

The whole ethos of performance must start at the top and be built into the strategy. In the opening chapter of this book Stephen Williams of ICL describes the commitment of his chief executive, Peter Bonfield, who in a statement to all employees wrote:

> By following the performance management processes, managers and their staff will be strengthening their working relationship and they will be able to maximise their joint contribution to the long-term success of the company. This will lead to a pattern of growth and achievement, providing good results for the company and a rewarding and satisfying working life for everyone in ICL.

Stephen goes on to describe how performance management is embodied in the values of the company as part of the ICL Way. The organisation has a *commitment to achievement* which unequivocally states that: 'Performance is the way forward – for every individual and for the company as a whole. It is therefore vitally important that every individual has a clear understanding of his or her work objectives and responsibilities, because performance will be measured against these.'

But if individuals are to be assessed on the basis of how well they have achieved their objectives, then those objectives must be both clear and agreed. If you don't know where you are going, how will you know when you have got there? Carol Whitaker, in her chapter on performance measurement, elaborates on this view. In her opinion, 'Measurement of performance in an organisation is at the core of any system of performance management. This is because, in order to evaluate and improve anything in life, we have to know from where we are starting, and how we are doing as time passes.'

Interestingly, Carol does not view the performance measurement process as simply being a benefit for the organisation; she believes that it, and the associated appraisal of performance, should also be established as part of an employee's personal development. Appraisal, in the guise of critical evaluation, is seen by Roger Holdsworth as being at once a uniquely human capacity and a major preoccupation of the species and, as such, a self-evident necessity. In his chapter on the subject, Roger traces the history of the appraisal process together with future trends; he looks at its inextricable links with performance measurement and salary reviews; and he puts the appraisal form itself firmly into perspective. It is clear that he has some sympathy with the academic who wrote that organisations considering the introduction of an appraisal scheme should wait a couple of years and concentrate first on developing the appraisal skills which would give a subsequent scheme at least half a chance of succeeding!

Returning to the theme of personal development which is addressed in earlier chapters, Roger also highlights its role in the appraisal process, suggesting that three of the questions that should be addressed during an appraisal ought to be: 'How can we work together more effectively to improve performance?' 'How does this job fit into the appraisee's broader career and life perspective?' And 'What action can be taken to develop the appraisee in this broader context?'

The answer to this last question leads neatly on to two other chapters in the book; the first on performance-related skills training and the second on coaching and counselling. Increasingly, organisations are beginning to realise that simply sending managers off on training courses does not necessarily achieve anything in terms of their personal development. Alan Mumford puts forward the view that 'the enhancement of performance through training is most likely to be achieved when the training itself is focused through performing real tasks of significance to those involved'. He also makes the point that any training must be integrated with experience; to be effective, there needs to be a process of continuous learning based on thought and reflection on both the managing process itself and the learning associated with it.

Managers necessarily need to have some responsibility for their own performance and for that of their subordinates. All too often the response to a development need is to send the person on a course. In reality, one of the most important features of a performance culture is that managers are ready and able to give feedback to their staff on a regular basis and that they can coach them in areas where their performance needs to be improved. In her chapter on coaching and counselling, Tricia Allison reminds readers that although company directors often *assert* that their most important resource is people, they rarely remember to protect, support and nurture this resource.

Coaching is based on the concept that individuals learn most from the everyday application of skills and by trying things out in practice. In Tricia's view coaching is a long-term strategy, but the rewards are greater job satisfaction, greater enthusiasm and improved performance. She also supports the view that the benefits of coaching are two-way, quoting Robert Townsend in *Up the Organisation*: 'Every success I've ever had came about because I was trying to help other people.'[3] According to Tricia, the skills used in effective coaching are communication, motivation, delegation, planning and monitoring – which are precisely those required to be an effective manager.

So, we can see that to build a useful performance management system we have to decide on our objectives; decide how to measure performance against these objectives; tell people how well they are doing; and give them the tools and the support and encouragement to improve their performance. To complete the cycle, performance must also be built into the reward system. However, performance-related pay, as Vicky Wright asserts in her chapter, is probably the most controversial element of performance management. Many people find the link between performance appraisal and pay an uncomfortable one. Yet in organisations where the culture has a performance orientation, performance-related pay is seen by employees as a more equitable reward system than those which offer no relationship to performance.

In her chapter Vicky brings all the negative arguments out on the table and deals with them objectively. At the end of the day her view is that performance-related pay will be a growing trend in this decade and that to be successful it must not be seen as a 'quick fix' but rather as part of an integrated performance management programme.

But reward is not always about money. People in organisations have traditionally looked to promotion as recognition for their performance. However, where levels of management are reducing, promotion is no longer a simple path; at times we have to be content with interesting sideways moves. In addition to this, the degree of change in the business environment means that skills can easily become redundant. From the organisation's viewpoint, and increasingly from that of the individual, there is a need to capture this kind of information in a readily accessible system.

In his chapter, Peter Wallum explains how succession management is a key element of the performance management approach. He asserts that it has benefits for the individual as well as the organisation and demonstrates clearly the links with areas such as recruitment, training and career counselling. He is also able to demonstrate some of the weaknesses of the conventional appraisal process: 'When the chips are down in terms of nominating people for possible appointments, quite different judgements are frequently made to those arising from the face-to-face discussions involved in appraisal.'

Succession management provides a very clear link between performance management and the business planning process. Peter gives examples where organisations have had to modify their strategic plans on the basis of information about the levels of skills and experience within the organisations.

This brings us back full circle to the opening chapter of the book, where Stephen Williams describes how no formal business review would be conducted at ICL without considering organisational capability. Indeed, this is known as the Organisation and Management Review and is the first item on the agenda of every quarterly business review meeting held by the chief executive.

In my own final chapter I have set out to demonstrate how the constituent parts of a performance management system are necessarily interlinked. There is often a feedback loop from one facet to the other. It is the role of the human resource specialist to facilitate the capture of this information so that it is fed back into the strategic and business planning process.

So the cycle is complete. It is a truism to say that organisations can only deliver their strategy through the people that they employ. Nevertheless, many employers have yet to recognise what this means in practice and do not acknowledge the complexity of the process. In this book the IPM has set out to demonstrate how the pieces of the performance management jigsaw fit together and to give examples of how organisations are dealing with the issue. The authors have amply demonstrated that, when a performance management system is operated effectively, there are great benefits for individuals, and organisations are far more likely to meet their business goals.

1

Strategy and Objectives

by Stephen Williams

Performance is the way forward – for every individual and for the company as a whole. It is therefore vitally important that every individual has a clear understanding of his or her work objectives and responsibilities, because performance will be measured against them – extract from *The ICL Way*

The words 'performance management' have over the recent past become some of the most overworked in the lexicon of personnel management. But what is performance management and how will it help your business? Is it simply a differential pay system, an objective-setting methodology or an appraisal process, or is it about career management? A true performance management system should comprise all of the above and, as a whole, will contribute far more than the individual elements alone. When operated successfully performance management will give the means for evaluating and improving both individual and company performance against pre-defined business strategies and objectives. Ideally, it will provide the basis for managing the business of today and for developing it into the future – *through the performance of its people*. As such, performance management should demand the attention and consideration of both the Chief Executive and the Personnel Director.

However, the real challenge of performance management does not lie in appreciating the value of the concept but in turning this understanding into a practical reality. These practical aspects can best be demonstrated by using a 'living' example to illustrate the key principles, benefits and issues related to performance management. The case study used is that of ICL, currently the most profitable IT company in Europe. ICL as an integral part of its business strategy put into place an interlocking series of attitudes, processes and skills to achieve continuing improvement in the effectiveness, productivity and development of its people.

This was the lever they chose for translating their business strategy into relevant, shared and implementable actions.

The ICL Experience

So how have ICL been able to achieve an effective performance management system that remains a fundamental part of the way all of its several thousand managers actually manage through their people? Was it just that they had a better process than many other companies? Was it that they managed to recruit managers over the years who naturally took to performance management? Or were there other factors?

Business Crisis

To begin to understand the answer we have to go back to 1980, when a series of factors – strength of sterling, inflation, interest costs and a cost base too large for a falling revenue growth rate – led to a business crisis in ICL. As so often happens in such circumstances, this very crisis forced a revolutionary look to be taken at how the company was operating and where it was going, in this case by a new top management team that included ICL's present Chairman and Chief Executive, Peter Bonfield.

New Business Directions

They determined that a totally new approach was needed to markets, to technology, to collaborations and to competition and that this new approach was needed fast in order to survive. They also soon appreciated that these new approaches would founder unless they were successfully implemented through the commitment, energies and skills of ICL's 20,000+ employees. They saw that an effective human resource strategy was required as an integral part of the new business strategy. To quote the new Managing Director:

> I gradually realised that I lacked the levers to transfer my strategic insight into the hearts and minds of the organisation so that they shared the imperative. They had to know why, not just what. An impressive programme of communication was not enough. I got immensely frustrated – thousands of bright people all working hard but not buying into the directions.

He is also reported as having used the well-worn saying of a

Second World War US general: 'I have seen the enemy and he is us.'

The Need for a Human Resource Strategy

He had come to the stark and obvious conclusion that the company's strategic thinking and its organisational capability were interdependent if ICL was to rise to the challenges and respond to the changes needed to survive, grow and prosper. He and his Board of Directors had come to realise the necessity of having a human resource strategy as an essential ingredient of the total business strategy. Further, he had come to realise that it was the management group who were key to the successful implementation of the company's strategy and it was this same group who were the prime shapers of the actual relationship between the company and its employees. What was needed was the creation of an environment and a framework within which managers could manage. As Peter Bonfield himself recalled:

> The prime people lever we chose to change attitudes was management capability. Of all the things which influence people's perception of what the company thinks is important, it's the way managers actually work that is most significant: the way they spend their time, the priorities they set, the languages they use, the standards they demand, consciously or unconsciously.

This visible level of commitment and leadership was an essential ingredient in creating the right environment for people management in general and performance management in particular to prosper. It enabled the first of three sequential initiatives to be launched in 1982. These were:

- the creation and communication of the *ICL Way* booklet
- the delivery of a Core Management education programme
- the definition and implementation of a set of people management processes which included performance management as the pivotal element.

Each of these initiatives was a vital ingredient in its own right, but it was their collective effect on winning the 'hearts and minds' of ICL's managers and employees that proved to be of crucial importance.

The ICL Way

Until 1982 ICL had made no statement of its values and beliefs and thus had never communicated these to its staff. This was the purpose of the *ICL Way* booklet which was distributed to all employees and is given to every new employee on joining the company. On the front cover, significantly, are the words 'The way we do things around here'. Inside are a set of *seven commitments* for all staff and *10 obligations* for all managers designed to set out the way that ICL means to run its business. It gives a shared vision of the way senior management wants ICL to be and how this would support the culture and the attainment of the business objectives and the business strategies. It also brings home to all managers the realisation that human resources are a prime source of competitive advantage, thus helping create the environment for effective performance management to succeed. It contains, for example, the assertion that:

> Our attitude to people is created by the fact that we are in a knowledge industry. Our business success will therefore be led by people first and products second.

Further, one of the commitments from the *ICL Way* was the *commitment to achievement* which stated:

> ICL is an achievement company. Recognition, rewards, promotion and opportunities for career and job development depend absolutely on results delivered. Performance is the way forward – for every individual and for the company as a whole. It is therefore vitally important that every individual has a clear understanding of his or her work objectives and responsibilities because performance will be measured against these. It is down to managers to make sure that these objecives and responsibilities provide maximum opportunities for the development of individual talent and to operate the company's recognition and reward systems on their achievement.

This belief lies at the heart of ICL's approach to performance management.

Management Education

The second of the three initiatives related to the Core Management Programme. At that stage it was a conscious decision to concentrate on education as opposed to management skills and training, which came later. The objective was to communicate the strategic vision and, just as important, the rationale behind it to the total management population in ICL. In turn this was intended to reinforce and put into context the relevance of the values contained in the *ICL Way*. This programme recognised that major shifts were needed in the way that people thought, made their decisions and conducted their lives in the company. It was, for example, designed to help people attune to the need to be marketing-led rather than technology-led; to be externally focused rather than internally orientated; to realise ICL needed to concentrate on target markets rather than try and do every-thing; and, above all, that ICL needed to *change* to succeed.

People Management Processes

Statements of belief on their own do not directly help managers do their jobs more effectively. Similarly, an understanding of the need to change and the associated strategic vision do not lead directly to the achievement of the required end result. As the third element, what was needed was a set of people management processes which would translate the *ICL Way* vision into reality and would enable employees to deliver the understood strategy in an effective and coherent manner. Peter Bonfield charged the personnel function with delivering such a programme which combined sound and straightforward processes with skills train-ing necessary for managers to ensure effective implementation. So was born ICL's Investing in People programme, a major element of which was a booklet entitled *Managing for Performance Through the Year*. This was a practical handbook explaining the processes, giving easy to follow examples and stating in unequivocal terms the requirements of each manager. Copies were given out at training sessions run by the in-house personnel function. In his introduction to the booklet Peter Bonfield con-firmed his own commitment and beliefs:

> Effective management of our people helps to answer the question: How do we implement our strategies more rapidly? By following the processes set out in this handbook, managers will be strength-ening the working relationships with those they manage and thus be contributing to the long-term success of the company.

In this statement he re-emphasised a key element of performance management, namely the manager/employee relationship. This aspect and others are perhaps best illustrated by giving an outline of the elements that make up the ICL performance management system.

The ICL Performance Management System

The process itself is not complex and, as Figure 1.1 shows, consists of a logical cycle of four steps linked with the company's business strategies:

- Step One   – The determination and *setting of individual objectives* which support the achievement of the overall business strategies
- Step Two   – A *formal appraisal* centred on what was achieved against these pre-agreed objectives. This results in the joint determination of a personal/job improvement plan, a career development plan and a training plan, plus the allocation of a performance rating by the manager
- Step Three – A separate *pay review* in which the level of pay increase is based largely on the actual level of achievement made against the pre-agreed objectives.
- Step Four   – An *organisation capability review* which, as part of the normal business review process, focuses on the total organisational capability of each part of the organisation to achieve the future business strategies.

The Principles of Performance Management

The introduction of the ICL performance management system required that the chosen process took account of certain principles. Some of these were behavioural, some of them procedural – all were practical rather than purely theoretical, as can be demonstrated by describing each of the four steps in the system in more detail.

Step One – Objective Setting

The setting of objectives is the management process which ensures that every individual employee knows what role they need to play and what results they need to achieve to maximise their contribution to the overall business. In essence it enables

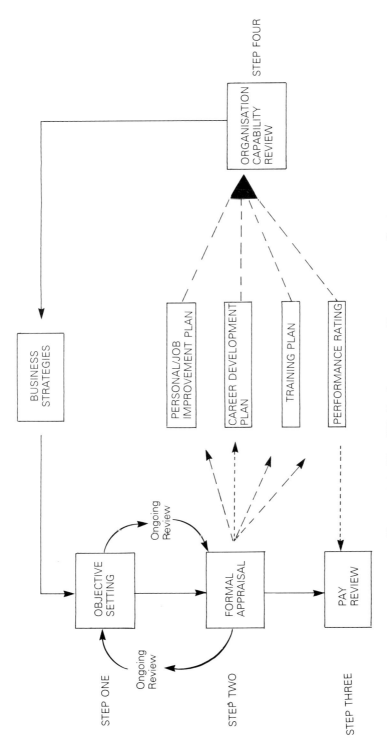

Figure 1.1: The ICL Performance Management System

employees to know in advance what is required of them and on what basis their performance and contribution will be assessed.

This requires that mechanisms are established which ensure the objectives:

- are jointly agreed in advance between the manager and the individual employee as both realistic and challenging and, as such, that they are 'owned'
- measure the actual level of achievement so that the basis on which performance is assessed can be understood in advance and is as clear as possible
- support the overall business strategies of the company so that the objectives, taken together, are mutually supportive and consistent throughout the organisation.

To achieve these three key principles the system uses a cascade process down the organisation from the very top through the four or five management levels. Typically it will take a month to complete the whole exercise for every single person in the company. Every manager, starting with the MD, holds an individual meeting with each of their 'direct reports' at which they discuss their objectives and jointly agree on their content and realism.

At these face-to-face meetings the rationale for the objectives in supporting the overall company business strategies is agreed, as are the specific measures that will be used to assess the actual level of achievement. Typically each person agrees with their manager six to eight ongoing objectives for the year. These are recorded and used as a working document by both the manager and the direct report at regular informal reviews throughout the year. Where appropriate, objectives are amended, deleted or added to as business requirements change. In this way objectives are not seen as rigid but dynamic, and as the means by which ongoing achievement is reviewed and controlled.

At the end of a 12-month period performance against objectives is reviewed as part of the formal appraisal process. Using this approach there should be no real surprises at the formal appraisal, as both the manager and the individual will have been regularly reviewing what has been achieved as part of the normal working process.

Effective performance management relies on effective objectives being determined. The acronym SMART is a useful guide in that objectives should be:

S pecific
M easurable
A greed
R ealistic
T ime-related.

In ICL all managers are trained in objective setting and shown how to develop objectives that consist of an *end result* (what will have been achieved) and an *indicator of success* (how it will be measured). They are shown that each indicator of success must relate to a measure of either quantity, quality, time, behaviour, resources or money. As an example, 'to provide a resourcing service to line management' is *not* an objective for a recruitment officer but only a statement of purpose for that job, whereas 'to provide a list of candidates to line management which meets the approved job specification within 15 working days' *is* a measurable objective.

Similarly, ICL managers are trained that there are three types of objectives:

- objectives which contribute to the achievement of the business objectives of the unit – *key result areas*
- objectives which contribute to an improvement in the performance of the individual job – *performance standards*
- objectives which contribute to the development of the individual – *performance development*.

The emphasis on the three different areas will typically vary according to the level and nature of the job and the individual's career development. A newly recruited graduate may well have a heavier emphasis on personal development objectives. An administrator or secretary who is operating processes may well have a predominant emphasis on job-related performance standards. A senior manager may well be set objectives where almost all the emphasis is on the achievement in key result areas.

Objective setting is a vital part of performance management but in reality is not a difficult process – provided managers know what they are trying to achieve and are prepared to devote some management time to defining this and to gaining the individual commitment of each direct report to the role they will play.

Step Two – Performance Appraisal

Performance appraisal is the review and discussion process which ensures employees receive feedback and assistance with their performance and development. It is based on the belief that fair and objective feedback assists individual development and helps improve performance. To make appraisal effective within an overall performance management system requires that mechanisms are established which enable:

- performance to be reviewed as an *ongoing* element to the mutual benefit of the company, the manager and the individual
- an *effective and reliable link* to be forged between the actual level of achievement made against the objectives and the reasons that contributed to this level of achievement
- *joint discussion and determination of supportive action plans* which are seen to be of mutual benefit in improving performance and personal development.

To achieve this, ICL managers use the ongoing review of individual performance as a tool to monitor progress against the business objectives of that activity. As such the dialogue between the manager and the direct report is real, related to the business and ongoing. In addition, a standard is laid down that a semi-formal one-to-one discussion between the manager and the direct report should take place at least quarterly. This not only reviews progress against the objectives but also on any previously agreed personal development actions.

The formal appraisal itself takes place annually and acts as a documented summary of the ongoing discussions that have occurred during the year. These centre on what was achieved and, just as important, the reasons for that level of achievement. To aid this process all ICL managers are provided with a descriptive list of about 30 criteria – a kind of shorthand of competencies – to help classify characteristics. Examples of these are initiative, adaptability, communication, delegation and planning.

As part of the formal appraisal process a number of these are selected by the manager as particularly relevant to why the level of achievement against the pre-agreed objectives was high or low. In this way the manager can help consolidate strengths and help the individual improve on relative weaknesses. In particular, managers are asked to discuss specific illustrations of the effective or non-effective use of that particular criterion in achieving or not achieving the objective. This encourages open discussion based on factual foundations rather than overly based on general-isations and unsubstantiated opinions which have little to do with the achievement of results.

The descriptive list of the criteria provided to managers also contains suggested ways of helping individuals improve this facet of their performance in terms of job content, projects, group activities or suggested reading. Thus the managers begin to fulfil the key role of 'coach' responsible for the development of their staff by providing on-the-job assistance rather than an immediate and often expensive recourse to formal off-the-job training.

Outputs from Appraisal

In ICL there are four specific outputs from the appraisal, three of which are derived from joint discussion and agreement, the fourth of which is determined solely by the manager. These outputs are:

- *the personal or job improvement plan* based on the principles described above and recorded as an agreed action plan. Such actions could include on–the-job training, coaching, reading, seminars, counselling, distance learning, projects, second-ments, etc.
- *the career development plan* which defines the most suitable job progression for the employee, taking fully into account the wishes of the individual and the needs of the business. Nat-urally it is important that agreed actions are based on an honest approach and are realistic, in that the manager must be able to implement or directly influence the result. The adage of not committing to something that the company cannot deliver is to be commended!
- *the training plan* which records the off-the-job training or edu-cation actions which support both of the above. In addition, any need for 'top down' business training, required to enhance the company's level of skills and knowledge, is defined. The plan will specifically record what training will be undertaken when and who is accountable for ensuring it occurs
- *the performance rating* which is the description which best sum-marises the manager's view of each direct report's overall per-formance against objectives over the preceding 12 months.

In this way the benefit of appraisal is increased by setting it within an appropriate context, by basing it on common standards and by supporting the individual in actionable terms.

Step Three – The Pay Review

The third element of the performance management cycle is the link with pay, which at first sight may appear the most obvious embodiment of performance management. In reality this is not normally the case and the scope and benefits of performance management go far beyond the pay mechanism (see also Chapter 5).

To be effective within the performance management context the pay review needs:

- to be strongly linked to the level of individual achievement in a way that can be demonstrated to be fair and logical
- to be relevant to everyone; many people will never be 'high-flyers', but they can still be committed to producing a sound performance against their objectives and receive a fair reward on this basis
- to be determined by the line manager of the individual within any overall company-determined pay guidelines, as it is the line manager who is in the best position to measure relative performance.

To achieve these aims, it is helpful to have a linking mechanism between individuals' performance and their level of pay increase. So, just as we have seen that performance criteria can help forge the link between an individual's performance against objectives and the personal improvement plan, the use of performance ratings can provide a similar link between performance and the level of pay increases. However, it is far too simplistic to believe that there should be a totally prescribed formula for making this translation.

In the ICL system, while it is fully recognised that the performance rating is *the* most significant factor that managers will take into account in deciding the level of pay increase, they will also consider the position of the individual in the salary scale, that person's recent salary history, the market value of that type of job and factors such as scarcity of skills.

The link between pay and appraisal and the use of performance ratings are discussed in more detail later in this chapter as both are important issues to be determined in line with the style of the individual company.

Step Four – Organisation Capability Review

The previous three steps have focused on the direct partnership between the manager and the individual and in this sense are free-standing. However, in addition the consolidation of all the individual outputs, and specifically those derived from the three plans which emanate from the formal appraisal, provide the basis for a review of the total organisation capability of that part of the company. In this context organisational capability relates to the ability of each activity to meet its future business objectives and strategies by considering issues of structure, people and management processes. This review considers whether the business objectives are in line with the organisational structure, with the required type and level of skills and with the need for adequate succession strength. Where there are gaps – almost inevitable when judged against the 'ideal' – the focus needs to relate to the training, resourcing, development and structuring plans to be met if the overall business strategies are themselves to be achieved.

Within the ICL context there is the absolute belief that no business plan or review is complete without considering organisation capability. This is known as the Organisation and Management Review (OMR) and takes place at each management level in the company, resulting in an upward cascade such that the Managing Director conducts an OMR with each business in ICL on a quarterly basis.

The OMR itself covers:

- *business objectives and strategies*, highlighting those objectives which depend for their achievement on organisation capability, for example a new vertical market impacting on skills, resourcing and training needs
- *organisation structure* which reviews any proposed changes to meet business requirements
- *career development* which reviews the senior staff of the business in question, together with their successors and staff with key skills or significant potential, and covers their career potential and development needs
- *strategic resourcing* which reviews any key resourcing issues that have a significant impact on the business and the proposed solutions
- *strategic training issues* which identifies longer-term training needs required to meet business needs.

In this way the OMR is formally linked to the regular business review process, and a powerful weapon has been added to the company's armoury. Within ICL it is seen as one of the major 'add value' roles of personnel activity and is in fact the first agenda item of every Quarterly Business Review undertaken by Peter Bonfield. Not at all surprising if one genuinely believes that people are the key differentiator for business success!

Issues to be Faced in Performance Management

The benefits of a proper performance management system – in developing employee understanding of what needs to be achieved and in helping all employees to improve corporate performance and be rewarded on the basis of that contribution – should be obvious. However, there are many issues to be considered in determining the most relevant way of implementing an appropriate scheme.

The Link with Pay

Perhaps the most pressing is the decision on how strong the link should be in the appraisal discussion between performance improvement, career development and the pay award. Some eminent personnel professionals would argue that these three elements of appraisal should be kept entirely separate as each may infringe negatively on the other elements. Others would argue that if one believes the level of performance should be a major factor in determining the level of career and monetary rewards, then the link should not be seen as too remote.

Within ICL the appraisal review does link a review of performance with a review of career development and does result in the award of a performance rating. However, this rating is a general indication of the level of achievement against objectives, and as such does not specifically define the level of monetary award in the pay review, which is carried out some time after. Obviously crucial factors in determining the right approach include the style of the organisation, the skill of the appraising managers and the level of training and assistance that managers have been given.

The Use of Performance Ratings

The linking of performance with pay requires consideration of the need for and value of performance ratings. Certainly rating performance either numerically or descriptively can be a sensitive issue. Equally, however, to forgo the use of performance ratings can severely weaken the link between performance and the level of pay increase that is awarded.

In this regard it is useful to express each performance rating in terms of the level of overall achievement made against the pre-agreed objectives. Thus one such definition could read 'The individual has met the objectives and requirements of the job, consistently performing in a thoroughly professional manner' while another could read 'The individual has not met many of the objectives or requirements of the job and needs to be helped to improve performance or to move to a more appropriate position.' Again the level of expertise is all-important, since managers need to be able to link the level of achievement against the objectives with the most appropriate performance rating and, most important, to explain the rationale.

Two key factors which should be emphasised in gaining the essential level of individual employee acceptance and motivation are:

- the use of specific examples of work performance and the ability to draw from them illustrations which help demonstrate the reasons why tasks were or were not achieved
- the genuine commitment on the part of the manager to provide practical assistance in developing employees' capability and contribution.

Both of these factors reinforce the need to provide 'skills' training for managers before the implementation of performance management systems.

Fairness and Consistency

A further issue often voiced is how a performance management system can be justified in terms of the fair and consistent application of standards of performance rating and pay award. Certainly no system can guarantee this, least of all a non-performance-based system that applies a common standard of reward irrespective of individual contribution – often the end result of collective bargaining arrangements! The level of expertise of the manager is again a key factor, but there are also techniques to help gain high levels of consistency. One such is to implement a system by which peer group managers discuss the performance ratings of their staff with their senior manager or between themselves prior to determining what the performance ratings should be. This allows individual managers to integrate standards across an organisation. Ultimately, however, as with all judgements of people, there are no absolutes; it should be clearly understood that performance management is no exception to this rule.

The Motivational Impact

A final issue for consideration is the level of motivation or demotivation that performance management can bring to an organisation or individual. Largely this has to do with perceived fairness and a genuine belief that the manager is acting in a helpful and realistic manner. In ICL over 80% of employees who completed the annual Opinion Survey indicated they wished to be rewarded on the basis of their individual contribution. Equally, over 80% of staff and managers indicated in an audit of the effectiveness of the performance management system that it brought real benefits to them. Certainly there will be cases in such a system that will lead to a level of demotivation, but if employees are treated as individuals and are genuinely assisted to achieve higher levels of capability and contribution there will be *many more* cases of positive and strongly motivated employees.

The Role of the Personnel Function

So far, the role of the personnel function has not been specifically discussed, yet the Personnel Director has five crucial roles to play in the introduction and implementation of performance management:

- in gaining the commitment of the Chief Executive to utilise performance management as a key strategy in achieving business objectives
- in defining the performance management processes applicable to the particular values, culture and strategic vision of that company
- in providing the training to managers in the knowledge, skills and attitudes required to implement the processes in a professional manner
- in communicating to all employees the mutual benefits and genuinely held company commitment to the process
- in monitoring and evaluating its implementation, particularly in the early years, to keep the processes 'on track'.

All these roles are vital contributions to be made by the in-house personnel function in assisting the enterprise to achieve business performance and growth through its people. In essence this is the catalytic role of the personnel function, and one it should not easily surrender to external consultancies.

Summary

Performance management is the integrated process of objective setting, appraisal and pay determination which supports the achievement of the company's business strategies. At an individual level it will result in action plans related to performance improvement, career development and training. All of these processes need to be operated by the manager of the individual employee and all need a level of management expertise in their effective application. This requires not only processes which clearly spell out to managers their role and what is expected of them but also the creation and implementation of a supportive training programme. Specifically, managers need to be assisted in mastering the skills of objective setting, of conducting appraisals, of coaching their staff and of facing up honestly and professionally to difficult issues of performance.

Equally, employees of a company need to be assisted to give commitment to the principles of performance management. This requires an understanding of the processes and the benefits to themselves and the company, plus an appreciation of the company's genuine belief in a system supported by honest and open discussion and application. Perhaps this is best summed up by Peter Bonfield in his introduction to a comprehensive communication to all ICL staff telling them about the processes:

> People are the key to our business success and their performance and morale are related to the effectiveness of the leadership and personal example provided by managers. By following the performance management processes, managers and their staff will be strengthening their working relationship and they will be able to maximise their joint contribution to the long-term success of the company. This will lead to a pattern of growth and achievement, providing good results for the company and a rewarding and satisfying working life for everyone in ICL.

Finally it should not be underestimated that it is this level of commitment and leadership that creates the environment needed to secure the very real benefits of performance management. If companies are to be successful, to excel in what they do rather than just compete, then the full capabilities of their employees must be realised and released into action as a specific business strategy. It is people that ultimately implement and achieve business objectives and to do this people need to know what is expected of them, to be helped to develop their expertise and to be recognised and rewarded for their level of achievement – that is what performance management is all about.

2

Measurement – The Foundation of Performance Management

by Carol Whitaker

If you don't know where you're going, any road will take you there – *Koran*

The Importance of Measurement

One sunny morning in the Rocky Mountains, two campers came out of their tent to see a grizzly bear thundering down the slope towards them. Terror-stuck, one of them started to run, but hesitated when he saw his friend stopping to put on his trainers. 'Run!' he yelled, 'Don't you know a grizzly can run faster than we can?'

'But I don't have to run faster than a bear,' said his friend, tying the laces. 'I only have to run faster than you.'

Which of them survived? Naturally, it was the one who understood performance measurement! He knew what the objective was and what standards were relevant to it. So he could see immediately what actions were needed.

The measurement of performance in an organisation is at the core of any system of performance management. This is because, in order to evaluate and improve anything in life, we have to know from where we are starting, and how we are progressing as time passes. It would be inconceivable to think of financial management without the foundations of management accounts; or of marketing management without the measurement of the market's size and structure; or of production management without output statistics. Equally, the management of people's performance can be effective only if it is founded on relevant and reliable information – which can only be derived from the measurement of their performance.

The importance of good performance measurement is illustrated by the logical model that

- *success* depends on achievement of performance targets
- *targets* are set against established performance standards
- *standards* are defined on the basis of *measured performance.*

The measurement of performance is, therefore, the foundation upon which performance management is built. If the foundation is flawed, the whole structure is suspect.

Precisely what should be measured in any individual organisation depends upon the nature of that organisation's business, and on the jobs of the people within it. What is important is to identify the considerations that should guide management in deciding what should be measured, how it should be measured and how standards of performance and targets for achievement should be assessed.

To do this you need to start with the recognition that the performance standards and targets set in any organisation are the product of a complex range of forces on the business. Some of the more important ones are shown in Figure 2.1, which demonstrates that although standards and targets are 'set' by a manager, business activity is driven by many forces other than the single function for which those targets are being set.

This is a simple demonstration of just one thing: every task in an organisation is only conducted to produce a response to the forces acting on the organisation as a whole. These forces are not the sole concern of top management. They are important to every employee, and each and every employee will perform better if the performance of the job done is understood.

Examination of the subject is illustrated from the recent experience of a dynamically changing life assurance and pensions company, Black Horse Financial Services (BHFS). Details which illustrate particular issues are also drawn from other organisations: MSAS (a freight company), House of Fraser (a retailer) and Nielsen (a market research company).

To identify the important guidelines for performance measurement, it is necessary to consider those aspects of an organisation's business which will have a great impact on its performance measurement system. These are:

- *the market* in which the organisation operates
- specific *corporate challenges* for the individual organisation
- identification of the *right population* for consistent measurement systems
- the involvement of *people* as a key business asset.

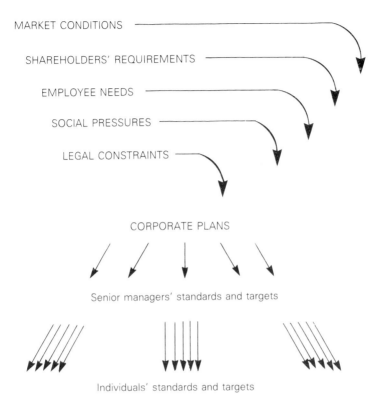

MARKET CONDITIONS

SHAREHOLDERS' REQUIREMENTS

EMPLOYEE NEEDS

SOCIAL PRESSURES

LEGAL CONSTRAINTS

CORPORATE PLANS

Senior managers' standards and targets

Individuals' standards and targets

Figure 2.1: Forces Acting on Performance Standards

These subjects have to be considered in order to avoid the naive view that Management by Objectives simply requires a manager to clarify what needs to be done in order to be able to get on and do it. The man who didn't put his trainers on learned painfully that knowing the goal (in his case survival) wasn't enough. Equally, in a business organisation it would be fatal to set the goals without establishing measurements. The result would be employees telling their managers: 'Well, I've achieved it by my standards. You didn't tell me what yours were.'

The question to ask is: 'Do your employees understand what you, the management, are trying to do?' There is a simple way of finding out. Talk to the people who do the work; ask what they do; how they feel about it . . . and then ask *why* they do it. If they do not know, it is no reflection on them. It is an indication that you have not communicated enough to them.

Communications will recur as a key element in establishing the best performance standards for the measurement of your business and for establishing a data set that can be used for analysis and targeting.

In building a data set, remember the key guideline to observe in developing performance standards: to be of maximum use they have to be measurable *over time*, so that change can be evaluated and analysed. To return to the parallels with financial, marketing or production management: the data sets on which their information is based also need to be interpretable over time. How could marketing managers cope with monthly or quarterly market research information that expressed their products' sales as a share of a market which is defined differently for every report? They could not, and no more can performance measurement be useful if it is calculated with constantly changing definitions.

Time should be spent addressing the question of what are the best and most relevant definitions for the measurement of a business. Of course, this is not an argument for a Jesuitical approach which can lead to 'analysis paralysis'. If you spend so much time searching for the Holy Grail of the 'perfect' measurement system that action is impaired, you will be defeating the object. It is as well to keep in mind that shambolic activity will always be more productive than ordered inactivity.

And, equally clearly, standards can and should be developed, modified or changed as business needs demand; the vital role of feedback is the subject of Chapter 8. But it should never be forgotten that large or frequent changes to the performance standards being measured will undermine the value of the very data set you are trying to improve.

Market Orientation

While it is usually clear that an organisation should be market-oriented in setting the standards by which its *corporate* performance is judged, it is not always recognised that market orientation is critical in judging employees' performance in *all* parts of the organisation. The difference between the two positions is demonstrated in the fashionable emphasis in many businesses on customer care. While the emphasis has been strongest in service industries – whether they are targeted at consumers or at other businesses – it is now an important consideration in many other industries too. This focus on customer care recognises the need to identify and respond to customers' expectations of organisations if they are to survive and to prosper. It is a prime example of market orientation.

Unfortuantely, the responsibility for customer care is too often vested in a single part of an organisation and is reflected in the performance standards only of that part of the organisation. Frequently it is marketing or sales. Such an approach fails to understand the full impact of customers on a business.

If customer care is to be the exclusive responsibility of just one function, it should be that of the Chief Executive! For it is the whole business which is affected by its position in the marketplace and by its customers' attitudes to it. It is not solely the marketing department's or the sales department's problem.

MSAS understood this when, in the mid–1980s, they were knitting together four different freight forwarding companies with widely varied backgrounds and cultures. They established a customer care programme for every single employee in the group, focusing on the needs of all customers – whether paying customers outside the company or interdepartmental customers within it. As a result, all employees began to understand far better how they could affect the services the company offered.

Such awareness of your customers' needs and your marketplace should be present when developing performance standards. This philosophy can be linked to the approach (promoted by the American Management Association) of the Unit President Concept. Briefly, this advocates that an optimum culture can be created if all managers in an organisation are directed to act, and encouraged to act, as if their units were separate companies, with the manager as President or Chief Executive. This approach brings an increased awareness of customers, both internal and external.

Figure 2.2 illustrates two different examples. The first is a chain of companies which service end consumers; the other is a single company. If the Unit President Concept is practised, market orientation is as likely to occur naturally in the performance standards of each departmental unit in the research company as in the separate companies of the razor blade chain. Moreover, it is certain that a market-oriented philosophy for the setting of standards will be understood and accepted in all those departmental units.

Figure 2.2 The Different Departments in a Small Company Parallel the Different Companies in a Group

This approach has to be understood by and reflected in the targets of all parts of an organisation if the business is to be truly focused on its customers. Furthermore, understanding of a marketing philosophy throughout an organisation requires thorough two-way communications. Management need to research and understand the way in which both their customers and their employees perceive their business; and they need to convey to both their awareness of their customers' needs and how they aim to meet them.

Again, we see that communication is important and it will recur. But for the present it is sufficient to recognise that, to establish the importance of performance standards in any organisation, a prerequisite is an understanding of the market environment. The principal case material relates to BHFS in the life assurance and pensions business, and (to practise what is preached) we should understand something of this market.

During the late 1980s the British Financial Services Industry underwent a revolution, being hurled from a relatively insular environment to a fiercely competitive one. Government action provided a major impetus. The 1988 Financial Services Act was stimulated by twin Government aims: to protect consumers and to encourage choice. Its provisions created opportunities for multi-service offerings and created more (and therefore much fiercer) competition.

Historically the life assurance and pensions sector of the market was fragmented, with several hundred companies providing services. Many were small and had a tough time coping with the new regulations, so that there was a consequent reduction in the number of small companies. Nor were the big companies immune from change. Mergers, like that of the Lloyds Bank interests in the market with those of Abbey Life, or the purchase of Scottish

Mutual by Abbey National, were not the only symptoms of change. Competition within this specialist sector of the financial services industry led the biggest parent organisations to operate their subsidiary companies much more autonomously than in the past, as Lloyds Bank did with their interests in the market. Simultaneously there were a host of strategic alliances where companies sought to tie up deals with the Banks and Building Societies who had a distribution network of branches and customers already in place.

Of course, the Boom-Slump-Recovery cycle that coincided with this period brought with it inevitable additional stresses – and singular failures like that of Prudential's venture into the estate agency business. Moreover, pressures on parent companies' businesses – such as the Third World and domestic bad debt provision forced on many banks – did not make life any easier either.

The life assurance and pensions sectors of the business were also adversely affected in 1989 and 1990 by a reduced property market, by increasing unemployment (which cut savings), by high interest rates, and by reducing private and public investment. These influences were coming to bear on a market that had seen enormous growth in the 1980s. An indication of this is the huge growth in new life assurance business which amounted to 119% between 1983 and 1990. But, by 1991, the sector was declining in real volume terms. Business value increased in 1990 by only 6%, and comparison with an inflation rate of over 9% indicated a 3% decline in the real size of the market.

Nobody at BHFS was immune from this market place and everybody's performance could only be judged in the context of the response to market conditions.

Meeting Corporate Challenges

BHFS performed better than the market during this period, but even with this success there were particular challenges in establishing suitable performance measurement throughout an organisation that was going through major cultural change.

Lloyds Bank has been in the Life Assurance business since 1975 when it set up Beehive Life, which became Black Horse Life in 1980, and BHFS in 1988. In 1988 it employed only 400 people (compared with 2,000 in 1991) but was already a rapidly growing business. With the 1988 Financial Services Act came the decision to 'polarise' service offerings within the Bank: that is, to change from a policy of branches acting as independent intermediaries in selling life assurance to one of active promotion of its own products.

In 1988, parts of the Bank's operations were merged with Abbey Life into a new company – Lloyds Abbey Life PLC, of which the Bank owns 60%. It has five UK companies in its structure: Abbey Life, BHFS, Lloyds Bank Insurance Services, Lloyds Bowmaker and Black Horse Agencies. Fully integrated operation of these units (whether desirable or not) is precluded by the 1988 Act which requires their separation and prohibits cross selling of directly competitive services that would inhibit consumer choice.

Lloyds Abbey Life, therefore, was faced with the challenge of developing two life assurance and pensions companies which could each benefit from a continuation of the historic strength of the two organisations. BHFS can be seen as gaining greatly. The injection of Abbey knowledge, skills and attitudes meant that their drive for a leading position in the market was to be based on an increased commercial awareness. Their strategic focus was increasingly to be on the development of a much more market-led and sales-oriented culture than they had had in the past. They were to be particularly concentrated on Lloyds Bank and Black Horse Agencies customers in response to the Bank's decision to polarise 'in-house'.

BHFS was strikingly successful in developing its businesses compared with the real decline in the market. In 1990 BHFS increased its Lloyds Bank business by 39% and profits by 57%. Over a longer time period too, it stood up as a notable success in comparison with its competitors. Only three years after the Lloyds Bank decision to polarise (which was critical to Black Horse being a serious contender in the market) it had established a 2% market share. In this fragmented market, where the market leader has only 7%, that was a substantial achievement, putting BHFS well into the top 20 UK companies. In 1987 it had struggled to be in the top 50.

Such success was not achieved without substantial changes within the company. Fundamental was a cultural change for the established employees of the original Black Horse Life which, as a subsidiary of Lloyds Bank, had enjoyed employment conditions, career development and appraisal policies rooted in the Bank's management culture. The need to move to a preferred, more sales-oriented culture was at the heart of the Lloyds Bank decision to incorporate them into a new public company, managed separately, even if it was 60% owned and used Bank branches for distribution.

The scope of the changes faced by BHFS was extreme: a planned shift in the way the company did things, a redirection of its business and the challenges of extreme growth combined with a difficult market and the need to structure operations to higher quality standards. Any organisation with vitality will be familiar with such changes. You do not even have to be market-oriented to recognise their inevitability; it was Mao Tse Tung who said: 'The only constant is change.'

Inevitably change is driven from the top of the company and the setting of performance standards must reflect top management's requirements at every level. But this is not simply a process of handing down directions. It is an iterative and evolving process.

At BHFS a crucial element in establishing the necessary two-way communications was the establishment of a formal process to review employee attitudes. The programme was conducted by professional market researchers and included in-depth qualitative research based on group discussions, followed by quantitative surveys of all employees. Awareness of the company's goals indicated the degree to which top-down communications was working. Moreover, the research provided an invaluable channel for assessing employee attitudes to the company's business aims and performance, and of their attitudes to:

- pay, benefits and conditions
- training, development and appraisals
- teamwork
- management style
- communications.

This sort of information is vital feedback in reviewing the effectiveness of the existing performance standards and how they should be developed. Particularly in the BHFS environment of change, with expanding staff numbers, the contrast in attitudes between newer employees and longer-established ones was helpful. Once such information is available as part of an organisation's management information system it is difficult to see how effective targets could be set without it.

Formal research is only one of several ways of gaining input from employees; others can be:

- project teams on key strategic issues
- quality circles
- suggestion schemes

- comments received through appraisal
- management briefings.

It cannot be emphasised too strongly that the communications must be two-way, and that they are not restricted to management passing information to employees on what is being done within the organisation. It is also imperative that management lets employees know how their comments are being used. There is nothing more motivating for employees two or three levels down the organisation than to sit in on a management briefing with colleagues and bosses, and to hear their boss explain how a modification of the corporate plan has been derived from information provided or analysed by them. And there is nothing more demotivating than hearing their cherished ideas adopted by superiors as if they were their own.

Naturally, management must talk about relevant parts of the corporate plan to the employees. Why should they not? If the employees do not know what they are aiming for, how can they achieve it? There is no corporate plan that is so dependent on secrecy that parts of it cannot be shared at every level of the company. Not that all staff will be interested in or want to know everything; but they ought to want and need to know the key signposts that signal the route that is being taken. Much of what they need to know will already be in the annual report if the company is public. But do not expect them to read it – they need to be told how it affects them.

Why is this two-way communication important in the context of setting standards and measuring performance? Essentially, it is because the standards for performance measurement throughout the organisation need to be relevant to business aims and – no matter how structured the systems for setting standards throughout the organisation – there will always be latitude for individual managers to take decisions on how to target their own area. Managers must be thinking in terms of the total business aims in choosing the standards that are to be applied within their own units.

At BHFS a programme of quarterly briefings and periodic management seminars led the communications programme. The seminars were known by the acronym QuEST, standing for Quality Excellence Service and Teamwork, which were the imperative qualities for the company's culture identified through the corporate planning process. Key results from these seminars were printed for wider distribution and for use by management in working with their staff. The seminars and the quarterly management briefings operated in two principal ways:

- *as a platform for management to explain plans* and to quantify the company's aims in terms that were specific and relevant to their audience.

   Figure 2.3 shows the key elements of BHFS corporate targets. When shown to staff it provided the sort of global background that was necessary for the subsequent addressing of specific subjects relevant to the audience.

- Achieve a growth in profit above 25% per annum, from the sale of life assurance, pensions and investment products to the customers of Lloyds Bank and Black Horse Agencies
- Treble our market penetration of this client base
- Enhance the bank/client relationship by the provision of a superior level of service

---

Figure 2.3 Key Corporate Objectives for Black Horse Financial Services

   Such subjects ran across the whole spectrum of the business because the whole business is relevant to all the management. They included reviews of budgets, recruitment processes, policy for employment terms and conditions, the introduction of job evaluation, product launches and so on.
- *as a forum for management participation in planning.* This must not be confined to questions and answers about the management presentation. It has to involve the whole audience. A route that is frequently used for this purpose is the establishment of working parties or project teams on specific subjects. At BHFS there were projects (emanating from QuEST seminars) on training and development, rewards and recognition, communications, quality and market image.

The vital thing about the whole process is that it has to be looped; that is, it must involve all parts of the business in the management task of developing plans and setting standards. QuEST teams were usually led by middle management, but included all levels of managers. They were under no illusions about the strategic priorities: they had been *told* what they were. If they went off the rails, there was always someone from senior management involved to haul them back on track.

   Reports of results were required to be specific about the aims and activities they recommended as well as the standards by which success was to be measured. Naturally, there had to be approval of recommendations, which was not always given without qualification. However, the plans which were finally accepted had the tremendous strength of being owned by the people who then had to manage them. The employees had set the standards to which they had to adhere.

Who should lead this communication process? Certainly, someone should have specific responsibility for it. At BHFS it is marketing who have responsibility for the subject, including newsletters, communications to bank staff, management briefings and so on. There is clear merit in such organisation of responsibility since it encourages a market orientation in the communication programme.

Measuring Different Populations

An interesting paradox emerges from BHFS's commercial success which demonstrates the dangers that can be inherent in establishing performance standards that are too bureaucratically consistent throughout a large organisation. What is at issue is not whether certain subjects that are key to an organisation should always be included throughout that organisation's performance standards and targets. It is the question of how regimented the measurements of performance should be against those standards, particularly when it is remembered that performance measurement is not an isolated subject but inextricably linked to other aspects of performance management, such as appraisal and reward.

BHFS was the most successful part of the Lloyds Abbey Life Group in 1990 – if the standards used are growth in business and profit. Such standards are inevitably high on any organisation's list, since it is on this basis that their owners or shareholders will judge performance. No less an authority than Cardinal Newman endorsed this when he wrote that 'Growth is the only evidence of life.'

Logically, then, the 1990 performance of BHFS's employees should have been reflected in relatively high appraisal scores compared with the Group as a whole. Paradoxically, this was not the case. The results for the 1990 appraisals showed that average scores elsewhere in the group exceeded those of BHFS. Superficially, this might be seen to indicate that something was wrong – with the standards set, the appraisal system or the training of managers – but this was not the case.

There were two key reasons for the occurrence of this phenomenon:

- *Growth expectations from the different parts of the group varied at the outset.* Since there was known to be great immediate potential in the BHFS business from a more commercial orientation, it would have been unreasonable to judge performance on an identical basis in all companies.
- *The people involved were different.* The individual companies were quite separate, so it was virtually impossible to have consistently applied systems. Varying attitudes and habits are bound to occur with different groups of people. For example, two different managers appraising an identical employee performance on a particular goal might say:

> Manager 1: 'That's as good as possible. Ten out of ten.'
> Manager 2: 'I never give top marks because perfection is impossible. Nine out of ten.'

Both positions are reasonable, and quite likely to occur. But they play havoc with comparabilities across an organisation.

Practical performance management must recognise that such circumstances will occur in many environments, and must accept that certain apparently illogical inconsistencies are quite insignificant (see also Chapter 4). The key point is this: while there are great benefits in having a consistent system for appraising performance across the whole of an organisation, relative performance against selected standards cannot be appraised with absolute consistency for different parts of the organisation and by different groups of managers.

The benefits of having consistent systems are felt by management and employees. Management can use appraisals effectively if they understand the process that produces them, and one process is simpler to understand than many. Employees who move from one part of the organisation to another will be more comfortable with familiar appraisal systems.

However, consistency of appraisals cannot be achieved unless there is a common management of the process. Bureaucratic processes might have to be in place for equalising the distribution of appraisal scores, to eliminate any disparities among them which reflected the attitudes or habits of different appraisers. Such bureaucracy can seriously reduce the credibility of a performance management system because what it says to the

employee is this: 'However your boss appraises your achievement of targets, your rewards will not be demonstrably in line
with that achievement.' This has to be avoided.

It is usually a simple matter to register those parts of an organisation where direct comparisons are valid and where they are not.
At the extremes, comparisons will normally be valid within a
single department, but they will not be between companies. They
will be easier within than across disciplines, and within rather
than across sites.

Within Lloyds Abbey Life, the individual operating company
is the largest unit where direct comparisons can be valid. In a
single company such as BHFS common management is assured
by the collective involvement of the board in previewing the
performance of units within the company, before appraisals start.
In this way standards and measurements are encouraged to be
consistent.

The identification of where in an organisation direct comparisons are valid is a crucial task. This is because of the inter-
relationship between performance standards, performance
appraisal and rewards. Any employee should be expected to
accept an appraisal that is demonstrably fair against a peer group
– where targets are set, appraisals are made and rewards are
earned (whether in pay, bonus, benefits or career development
opportunities) on a consistent basis. But resentment will occur if
another group is seen to benefit disproportionately because it is
thought to have been judged by lower standards, or given easier
appraisals.

In this context it is impossible to separate the issues of performance measurement from those of appraisal and reward (see also
Chapter 5). The golden rule has to be that performance standards
must be consistently set and appraisals consistently made for any
population that is to have its share of rewards determined by
relative achievement. In the case of BHFS there was no problem
in the disparity with other group companies, because the reward
pools of the companies were separate.

However, difficulties will arise where there are inconsistencies
within a population that shares a reward pool. A route to avoid
those difficulties is to keep populations small. A large organisation like Virgin that is structured into many small business units
can avoid many of the problems of managing multiple standards
of performance measurement. Many companies, though, have to
face the challenge that their business units are large.

In this situation it is preferable that the reward pool is allocated
on a waterfall basis. Rewards are allocated en bloc to major parts

of the business on the basis of their overall performance – to sales, production, finance and so on. Then there are further allocations down to those made on the basis of individuals' relative performance within populations where equitability of treatment can be managed conveniently.

A case which serves to illustrate how this approach can be used to avoid the bureaucracy of equalising standards and appraisals across sites or departments comes from retailing. In the House of Fraser stores, performance bonuses were paid to management staff but were predefined so that (at individual store level) the employees knew their rewards would be determined by their site's performance.

Another case occurred at Nielsen Marketing Research. In the early 1980s they were facing the problem of variable standards being applied to the performance of secretaries across the company. This was a classic case of 'Her boss is nicer to her than my boss. Why should she be paid more when she is doing less work?' Are there any organisations where it never occurs? The solution Nielsen chose involved standards being set (and appraisal conducted) by a single secretarial manager. The person for whom a secretary worked retained a key influence on the process since the bosses' assessments (as sole 'customers') were an essential input.

In these ways the necessity for regimented measurement systems and over-heavy controls on appraisal diminishes. Important departmental standards can feature without risk of disadvantaging or over-rewarding that department, and the use of performance measurement becomes more a valuable tool of the 'unit president' than a mandatory corporate discipline.

People Sensitivity

It is not merely a by-product of good performance measurement that employees should feel that they own the systems of measurement and the standards by which they are measured. The best performance systems are developed from the outset with sensitivity to employees' needs and expectations. It is difficult to conceive of an organisation whose performance does not depend on the quality of the staff that make it work. This is widely recognised in some industries. The popular phrase that 'Our assets go out of the door each evening' originated in the advertising business and has since been applied to many other services, yet every type of organisation should regard its people as a key asset. People may not be given a value on the balance sheet but they are as important an asset as the capital equipment that they use in their work.

And what an asset! The manufacturing equipment, the computers, the cars, the furniture – all the things that do have a balance sheet value can have their functions precisely defined. Their performance standards are defined in their specifications, and no owner of such assets would expect them to be capable of replacing each other. Furniture will not be expected to compute the company's accounts, nor manufacturing plant to carry salesmen to their appointments. People are more flexible. They can be made more productive not only in the quantity but in the scope of their activity.

In people's flexibility lies a danger which should be recognised in the development of a performance measurement system. The danger is the virus that infects most systems from time to time – moving goalposts. This disease is caused by an organisation having to respond to its environment; its symptoms are standards and targets that change too frequently. If it is not treated it can be fatal to effective performance management.

Any performance measurement system must allow management the flexibility to revise standards and targets. It is obvious that the markets in which managers operate do not evolve to the schedules of their appraisal systems. Managers must be capable of responding to change, and this will inevitably involve revision of the standards and targets to which they work. If they are having to respond to change, so too must their subordinates. But, as Michael Porter has pointed out, even to suggest change in an organisation can be seen as an act of disloyalty, and if managers are seen as disloyal to their staff, results will suffer. The trick is to have necessary changes reflected in standards and targets by exploiting the flexibility of the 'people asset', without falling foul of the moving goalposts virus. There is no guaranteed way to achieve this, but sensitivity to people's needs will help. The keys are in discretion and, once again, in communication.

- *Only change when it is really necessary*. It is not a pre-requisite for managers to be guaranteed coverage of all their goals by those of their subordinates. It is much more important that a team is kept motivated than that each and every minor accountability in a plan can be assigned to an individual. There may be more important things going on. Remember Lincoln's advice that 'It is not best to swap horses while crossing a river.'
- *Only change when there is time for the change to be effected*. To be

told in month 11 of a year that targets have changed would be disastrous. Periodic reviews of standards, targets and performance creates the environment where necessary changes can be discussed in good time – as the circumstances requiring them become apparent. Quarterly reviews were right at BHFS, but the frequency will depend on individual businesses.

- *Explain the reasons for change and seek support in identifying the ways that a challenge can be met*. Involvement will always be more productive than direction, and it is wrong to expect that employees will be aware of the need for change without being told. In extreme cases employees can be faced at appraisal with comments such as 'But you should have understood that such-and-such wasn't important any more. . .' Again, the review process will help avoid this.
- *Recognise that change needs resourcing*. The resources that are needed will depend on the challenge being faced, but they need not necessarily be additional equipment or staff, nor even additional remuneration for the individual concerned. Overt recognition, additional training or career development can often be sufficient. At BHFS a programme of appraisal training was unavoidably delayed but had to be completed on schedule. It was accepted that additional consultancy resource be used to recover the schedule without decline in the quality of the programme.
- *Distinguish between the original plan and the additions to it*. If new targets are necessary – and accepted as being so by employees – it is still important that performance is also measured against the original standards, even if this involves extra measurement work for a period. At MSAS, when a depot was closed in Birmingham and the workload transferred to other depots, the depot managers were measured for a period on both their original and revised workloads.

These approaches increase managers' ability to extend the scope of the functionality of their 'people assets'. Even more positive results will be experienced if the whole system that is used is designed to be people-sensitive in the first place.

If it is recognised that people are an asset, and a more flexible one than capital equipment, it will be clear that they also need more flexible performance measurement and assessment against targets than machines do.

The performance of a machine can be measured clinically, but there is risk that too clinical a measurement of people's performance can be dehumanising. The challenge is for performance measurement, and the associated appraisal of performance, to be established as part of employees' personal development, and not as an annual test or a judgement. Here again, there are principles that can be observed that will make the system work better.

- *Distinguish between precisely measured standards and more subjective ones.* With certain aspects of performance it is important that standards should be unambiguous, measurement should be precise and targets should be absolute. It is obvious that a salesman's revenue target or a productivity goal in manufacturing should be precisely defined. But all employees will have some targets where measurement of their performance is more subjective. The quality of their personal development or contributions to extraordinary project work are areas where more flexibility can be observed in measurement of performance. If there are not absolute criteria for appraisal a manager should recognise this; and also recognise that erring on the side of generosity when it comes to appraisal will gain more in employee motivation than it will cost in precision.
- *Measure only what is relevant to each employee and target what can realistically be influenced.* While it was important that everyone at BHFS knew that the company goals included increased penetration of the client target, this could hardly be a performance standard that was relevant outside the sales and marketing divisions that are in a position to increase market penetration.
- *Include standards for personal as well as corporate development.* If the individual perceives the performance measurement system as being geared to personal needs there is a much improved chance of commitment to the system.

Performance Indicators

It is clear that a fundamental principle upon which professional performance management depends is continuous communication about performance. Whatever is being measured, and however targets are set, the employee will feel ownership of the system only if involved thoroughly in it on a continuous basis.

It is in this context – the continuity of communication – that performance indicators are important. Performance indicators for a job can be different from the standards of performance which are defined for it. Their purpose is to produce quick, simple and nonconfrontational measures of how things are going, so that the employee and manager can have a basis for reviewing progress. At managerial levels they will often feature in a monthly, weekly or daily report, and they will vary from performance standards because they will focus on causal information as often as results.

For instance, the key targets for a salesman will concern what is sold, and, of course, sales results can be measured at any time interval. However, an additional dimension can be added if the performance indicators used include the known *levers* that affect sales. If there is a known Call:Sale ratio for the business then a record of calls made will be a useful indicator of potential performance and an early warning system for potential problems.

The key factor in successfully using this tool is avoiding bureaucracy. Performance indicators form a basis for communication, not for appraisal. Their purpose defines their key characteristics, so they need to be:

- *quick to produce and present*. They describe how the job is going. Producing them should not be a job in itself.
- *simple*. They are headlines of a performance measurement system. They do not require perfectly rounded commentaries with them – they are only the basis for discussion.
- *Nonconfrontational*. Both parties should agree on their relevance to the job, but agreement is not paramount if their separation from performance standards is understood.

Once established, performance indicators can also prove useful in other areas such as job evaluation. Nielsen Marketing Research use the Hay system and incorporate in their job descriptions a list of the performance indicators registered against the accountabilities for a job. This was a valuable addition to their job evaluation system as well as that for goal-setting.

The Role of Personnel

Whether establishing a new system or adapting an existing one to a new environment, managers are faced with change, with developing something new – which is the biggest management challenge there is and always has been. As Machiavelli pointed out as long ago as 1514:

> It must be remembered that there is nothing more difficult to plan, more uncertain of success, nor more dangerous to manage than the creation of a new order of things. For the initiator has the enmity of all who would profit by the preservation of the old

institutions, and merely lukewarm defenders in those who would gain by the new ones.

Of course, Machiavelli was addressing a princely chief executive who did not have the benefit of a personnel department. With personnel at the helm it will all be plain sailing. Or will it?

Personnel functions have a key role in the development and administration of performance management systems but it must be recognised that this is a facilitating rather than a controlling role. It has been argued that personnel managers should have one constant goal – to work themselves out of a job! The point is this: personnel should always be striving to improve the quality of management of people, by helping other managers to perform better. The ultimate success (which, of course, they never attain) would be not to be needed at all, because the line managers in the organisation are performing perfectly.

This stimulating perspective has considerable relevance to the role of personnel in developing performance management systems. The personnel role is to help managers to manage performance better. Personnel will be involved in the design and development of measurement systems, in the training of managers to use them, in the scheduling of the periodic cycles of work, in counselling managers in their operation of the system, and in the analysis of results. At each of these steps the involvement must be that of a *support* to managers and never as a substitute for managers.

- *The design and development* of the system is the area where personnel are acting to support senior management's commitment to a performance management system. That commitment has to be there in the first place, even if it has been stimulated by personnel recommending performance management as a beneficial technique. Personnel should then involve all levels of management in assessing an optimum system for their organisation. And they will use that involvement in the design of their system. The same approach should apply to the evolution of the system over time.
- *Training* involves the whole of the company in understanding how they can operate the chosen system to their individual and collective needs. It is a key part of the communication programme, and personnel will be involved in it. To avoid being too directive in training, it is a good idea to have some of it carried out by the managers who have been involved in the design.

- *Scheduling* is the nearest that personnel gets to a line responsibility. It is likely that some policing will be needed to ensure that the system is operated to schedule. This will be particularly relevant in the early years of operation. It will take time for all staff to support the system and feel that they own it. Until then there will be cases where managers do not give sufficient priority to the exercise, and this tendency has to be resisted. Once the system is well established this job will become less onerous.
- *Counselling* is a vital part of personnel's work and one where there is the greatest risk of overstepping the mark. Circumstances can arise, for instance, where a manager will wish to modify a performance standard to better suit specific department needs. Reference is made to personnel: is the change OK? Assuming that the standard involved is a vital one that should not be changed, there are two possible scenarios:

Personnel say: 'No. That's a key standard. You can't change it.' The manager goes back to the department and says: 'Sorry. Personnel say No.' Result – employees lose commitment and see personnel as uninvolved bureaucrats if not ogres.

Personnel discuss why the standard concerned is key to the organisation and help the manager to identify how it can be maintained. The manager goes back to do the same with the department. Result – the employees retain commitment and the manager sees personnel as a helpful consultant.

- *Analysis of results* is another key element of personnel involvement. It provides the basis for review of the system and subsequent evolution (see also Chapter 8). Analysis of results is also closely involved with the link to rewards and identifying those populations where application of standards and appraisal of performance has been consistent. Here, as with the design and development of the system, personnel's function is particularly to be supportive of senior management in the organisation. An appraisal of the appraisal system proved useful at BHFS. Workshops on how the process went – from performance measurement through to appraisal – provided an effective feedback loop.

This philosophy of the personnel role in a performance management system is totally compatible with the Unit President Concept. If unit managers see themselves as the Chief Executive of their units, they will also see themselves as being responsible for all aspects of their unit's work – operating standards, customer care, finance, people, equipment and so on. They will be using the organisation's personnel function as a professional consultancy – and one from which they have a right to receive a service because they are paying for it, usually as an overhead charge. They will get value for money if personnel are helping them to observe the guidelines that have been established for professional performance measurement, and indeed for performance management as a whole. Figure 2.4 shows a summary checklist of 20 questions that should all be ticked if your measurement systems are in good order. The organisation will benefit most where everyone owns the system. The personnel function, too, will benefit from hiding its lights under a bushel. As La Rochefoucauld said, 'The height of cleverness is to be able to conceal it.'

Performance Measurement Policy

1 Is performance measurement the foundation of your performance management system?
2 Do your measures reflect the forces acting on your organisation?
3 Are your measures usable over time? Are their definitions consistent?

Market Orientation

4 Do your employees understand your market environment.
5 Do they understand the impact they have on your performance?
6 Is their impact on internal and external customers measured?
7 Do you research your customers' and your employees' attitudes?

Corporate Orientation

8   Is there a structured, two-way communication programme?
9   Is responsibility for the programme allocated within the organisation?
10 Do your employees understand your business aims?
11 Are employess involved in developing measures, standards and targets?
12 Is employee contribution overtly recognised in feedback?

Different Populations

13 Does your rewards system distinguish between comparable and non-comparable populations?
14 Are similar functions comparable across the organisation?

People Sensitivity

15 Do you distinguish between objective and subjective targets?
16 Are your measures relevant to individuals?
17 Do you include standards for personal development?
18 Do you restrict changes to a limited number of vital ones?
19 Are changes given time for, resource for and recognition of achievement?

Performance Indicators

20 Are your measures quick, simple and nonconfrontational?

Figure 2.4 A Health Check for your Performance Measurement System

3

Performance-related Skills Training

by Alan Mumford

Introduction

To some readers it may seem odd that skills training could ever be other than performance-related. The intention of this chapter is to show that some skills training for managers and professional people can be very little related to required performance. It then goes on to show why this can happen, and proposes two different strategies for ensuring that training is indeed directly related to performance.

The prime reason why skills training may on occasions not be related to performance is that it is quite possible to design and implement a programme which develops skills, but for those skills to have no direct link to what is either desirable or achievable within the organisation in which the learner works. The skill may not in fact be 'needed' in any except the most abstract sense, because the person does not currently have (and has little chance in the future of having) a need for the skill developed. For example, for some time I ran apparently successful courses on Chairmanship in an organisation where I worked. There was an increasing demand for the course, caused by complimentary post-course feedback. The course undoubtedly developed skills of chairmanship – the problem was that a large number of participants were not actually chairing meetings.

An even more frequently encountered problem, felt particularly strongly by participants, arises when the skills developed on a programme have no chance of implementation within the reality of the organisation. So, for example, in the heyday of the Organisation Development movement, managers and others were encouraged to develop the skills of openness, trust and effective confrontation through OD events – only to find that the organisation they were trying to develop had no intention of rewarding such skills.

Clearly, the appropriate way of avoiding such problems is to ensure that any training undertaken is derived from a large-scale and effective review of business needs. This is the view taken by many successful and relatively sophisticated trainers. There is, however, an alternative strategy, which can be described as the opportunistic approach. While similarly dealing with the realities of organisational life and specific development needs, it is essentially individualistic in style and purpose. The two strategies can be summarised as follows:

The Diagnostic Strategy
This involves a review of organisation purpose and plans. The skills, knowledge and attitudes necessary for the effective pursuit of organisational goals are identified. An audit of the extent to which staff currently meet the requirements is carried out (either at an organisational or individual level). Priorities are identified and skill-focused training is set up.

The Opportunistic Strategy
This strategy takes the reality of managerial life as the starting point. It assumes that while the diagnostic approach will present admirable and clear analytical processes for identifying performance requirements, managerial life tends to revolve around a dynamic of fluctuating and changing managerial priorities and incidents. This strategy accepts that managers are often driven by pressing immediate circumstances and priorities to develop their own skills, and to propose the enhancement of the skills of others. It accepts the reality of the often repeated managerial claim that most learning is learning from experience. However, the new thrust of management development in the '90s is to convert this clichéd image of managerial life into something more than an unthoughtful, unplanned series of experiences which may develop skills.

While the emphasis of most trainers to date has been on the more effective development of diagnostic processes, the two strategies need not be held in opposition to each other. Indeed, the reverse; they ought to be designed as an integrated total process for development. The reasons for this will be indicated in the specific cases developed later in this chapter. While the whole shift to performance-related skills training depends on the successful identification of performance criteria, it is by integrating the two strategies that we can ensure that *all* opportunities to develop skills for performance are identified and satisfied, rather than only those generated through a diagnostic process largely owned by personnel professionals.

Skills, Competences, Behaviours

Traditionally, trainers and educators have distinguished between skills, knowledge and attitude. This distinction has been helpful in the past because it contributed to clarification of the problems trainers were attempting to resolve. A personnel practitioner might need to '*know*' the Employment Protection Act 1978. Methods appropriate to delivering that knowledge, however, might well be different from those appropriate to changing *attitudes* about 'the right way to do things in making employees redundant'. This in turn is different from the *skills* involved in actually dealing with people who are to be made redundant.

More recently, the training and education lexicon has been supplemented by a focus on 'behaviours' – those things which people *do* and which, of course, represent a wide range of skills. So the disciplines of behaviour analysis have evolved, and subsequent processes of behaviour modification, and the requirement to spell out behavioural objectives on training courses. Of course, knowledge, attitudes and skills all contribute to exhibited behaviours.

In the world of management training, the newest word is 'competences'. Originally given attention by the major work of Boyatzis[1] in the United States, in recent years it has been given a major push in the UK by the Management Charter Initaitive and the statements of Competencies and Standards for management this has produced. There are a number of issues about competences in relation to performance-related skills training. Perhaps the most important is that there is likely to be an inherent conflict between the attempt to set nationally agreed standards of management competence, and the actual requirements of managers in particular organisations. The more generalised the statement of competence, the less likely it is to be actually relevant to an individual manager in any particular organisation.

The second issue is that it has become increasingly clear that the focus of the national competency movement is on the production of competences and standards which can be assessed in relation to a managerial qualification. The problems arising from this concern both the processes of assessment (not yet addressed at the time of writing) and the inevitably rather static nature of the assessment (as compared with the dynamic reality of management). A further complication is that it will necessarily involve an emphasis on literary skills rather than the direct skills of management.

Finally there are the issues of what competences are supposed to mean and cover – embracing, as they often seem to, a combination of skills, knowledge and attitudes. For these reasons it seems unlikely that the competency movement will satisfy the demands for enhanced attention to performance, except where they are made organisation-specific and where any educational qualification is seen as a side product rather than a prime purpose of the process.

The Diagnostic Strategy – A Case Study

In the mid–1980s Ford of Europe decided to make major changes to its organisation structure and management style. With Peter Honey and other colleagues I worked with the Product Development Group in helping them to carry out the changes required. The structural change was the adoption of a form of matrix management, in which complete car programs became the organisational base instead of the previously separate functional processes. The other major shift was away from what were described as traditional Ford styles towards a more participative management style.

The approach adopted was based on the view that any attempt to improve the ability of managers in Ford to carry out the new business-led requirements should derive from diagnosis of the particular Ford situation and requirements, not from traditional lists of skills of participative management. Second, we suggested, and gained acceptance for, the traditional training view that training would be more effective if it started at the top.

In order to establish both the context and the particularities of the required skills for matrix management, a number of topics were put to the 24 most senior managers in London and Cologne. Examples of topics discussed were:

- What do you understand by 'autocratic' and 'participative' in the Ford context?
- What progress and problems have you experienced in attempting to carry through the new principles agreed?
- Consider the managerial behaviour of your bosses: what do they do that helps or hinders you in the effective performance of your job?

- Consider your own managerial behaviour: what kinds of behaviour are rewarded, not rewarded, punished?

The data produced by these individual discussions covered a much wider field than the content of the programme described in this case. For present purposes, the most significant difficulties they had experienced included:

- There was disagreement about the meaning in operational terms of words like 'participation' and 'consensus'
- While the nature of approved managerial behaviour had been clear and consistent (although not articulated before), the nature of the 'now desired' managerial behaviour was not wholly clear and had not been articulated.

In addition to reporting data from the discussions, a number of other issues were identified, of which the most relevant for this chapter were:

- the need for a clearly stated and agreed definition of decision-taking processes
- the definition and acceptance of now desired managerial behaviour such as openness, confrontation, explicit feedback.

Involvement of the top management group is so often the unachieved Holy Grail of trainers. In this case the top management team is to be complimented for taking direct responsibility for improving their own processes first, instead of simply approving training for managers below them (which had initially been the brief). The top team participated in a two-day workshop which had four objectives:

- It should deal with the issue of clarifying terms
- It should result in a clear action plan for implementing the change strategy already decided
- The workshop itself should use the decision-making process suggested for the new structure. Decisions in the workshop would either be communicated by the Vice President ('I tell') *or* he would create discussion and share responsibility for the decision ('I share'), *or* he would create a situation in which the decision depended on full agreement by all participants ('We all agree')
- During the two-day workshop the top management team should tackle some of its normal agenda items in order to test

and validate the processes which the workshop was designed to encourage.

Peter Honey and I acted as Designers of the workshop, as Presenters during it and as Process Consultants to facilitate workshop activities. It will be seen that the design of the workshop explicitly addressed the performance management requirements for this particular group of top managers in this specific organisation.

Two elements not covered so far need to be emphasised. First, the use of real issues was not confined to practical work on the particularities of matrix management, but included significant agenda items on technical and financial issues. Second, the design of the workshop was explicitly related to the Learning Cycle, and even more specifically designed through the Learning Styles Questionnaire.[2]

This attention to the learning design was required for two reasons. While the use of the Learning Cycle can improve the design of any event, the application of individual learning style results is especially useful in creating a particular process for a specific group. In this case, the group's predominant style was Theorist. An additional reason is that the greater the reality of the experience to which managers are exposed, the greater the risk that they will be wholly consumed by attending to the task, and not using the task as well to understand how and why they are learning.

The success of this workshop for the top team led to the request for workshops designed for the remaining managers in PDG. Eventually, somewhere around 400 managers attended workshops in the UK and Germany. The major design features of these workshops again concentrated on the actuality of what the managers were required to do. In other words, they were required to work on the real tasks of defining Program Management, and specifically the skills involved in effectively carrying out the new managerial requirements. One important issue of principle was that we dealt with the actual Program Management teams, as compared with the alternative of mixing people across teams. The decision here was based on the view that it was preferable to deal with real issues in real terms, rather than simulating the work environment. Each group had the same basic requirement and went through the same process. Participants were given a short briefing session introducing the tasks for the workshop and supporting documentation. They then worked to produce their own statements of the behavioural skills necessary

to ensure the success of Program Management, and wo̵ː
the decision-making styles identified by the top managen̵ː
group in the first workshop.

The skills which they had identified as desirable for the totality
of Program Management were then in part deployed through the
requirement that each group make a 15-minute presentation on
the actions they proposed to take. They experienced not only the
actual deployment of the skills they had described as theoretically
desirable, but the difficulties they encountered in doing so.
Finally, each individual member had to develop an action plan
of activities that she or he would undertake when back at work.

The successful achievement of a task would not in itself have
produced the full potential benefits of the workshop. Individuals
and groups could get even more if they were helped to review the
process they had been through. So they were given an additional
'reviewing' task which required them to undertake this with
some help from a facilitator present in all groups.

It will be noted that again the 'double value' formula was used,
which is to pose real tasks within the Program Management
context, rather than the more familiar training process of invent-
ing unreal tasks for the participants to undertake. Identifying,
clarifying and negotiating the skill required, using the decision-
making processes involved and then reviewing how effectively
they worked in groups were more testing but, in our view, more
effective processes than simply presenting a list of skills and
providing some simulated experience of working on them.

It is not, for example, very difficult to get intelligent managers
to 'accept' that effective listening is a skill required if the aim is
to get effective participation (and is clearly less required if the
management process is authoritarian). However, people learn
more if they have to listen to other people describing what effective listening is, and then reviewing how effective they have been
in listening to them.

Case Study 2 – Using Opportunities and Problems

This case study draws together experiences in working with
directors in three organisations: Pilkington plc, Scottish Hydro
Electric plc and Swan Hunter Shipbuilders Ltd. Although in each
case the programme was specific to the particular organisation,
with the result that there were some significant differences in the
issues addressed, there was substantial similarity in the nature
of the work undertaken to meet performance requirements. Two

cases involved dealing with the needs of a complete Board of Directors, in the first a more diverse group of directors across a large organisation with subsidiary companies. In each case the driving force was essentially a recognition that changing demands on these organisations required changes in the type and level of performance required by directors.

The starting requirement, therefore, was to determine what the job of the individual director (and in two cases the job of a board) actually was. There are now some statements about what directors should do, and a traditional management development process would have taken such a statement and developed a programme around it. One view of what directors at corporate rather than functional level need to be able to do was indeed identified in my own research:[3]

- identifying strategic direction
- taking a corporate view rather than representing a functional division
- absorbing and recalling quantities of data without losing sight of main issues
- planning the future more than managing the present
- managing external relationships
- operating effectively in different organisational and national cultures
- influencing directors as powerful as yourself
- getting others to act rather than doing it yourself
- building relationships with non-executive directors.

It would have been quite understandable (and certainly relatively speedy as a process) if the organisations concerned had taken such a list, checked which items applied to them and asked for a programme which concentrated on the most important – perhaps supplemented by their own views. While no doubt each business school professor or consultant will have their own preference for a particular list of director-level skills, the idea of working from a research-based list of apparently general application is understandably attractive. The organisations mentioned in this case study, however, decided to use a different process. Instead of starting from a list of generally accepted skills, they engaged in a process which started by looking at the opportunities and problems faced by people directing the business. As in the first case described above, the business requirements had to determine the skills training which would be offered. However, whereas the Ford case revolves around one (although major) requirement for managers – the introduction of a particular management organisation and style – here there was an intention to cover much more of the totality of the requirement for effective performance.

The analysis of needs, therefore, started with the identification of views about problems and opportunities facing directors. In the case of the boards of Swan Hunter and Scottish Hydro Electric, those problems and opportunities were identified individually by the directors; in the case of Pilkington, they were identified by a representative sample of directors. Only after the problems and opportunities had been identified were directors asked to look at their own experience and their own skills and to relate these to the problems and opportunities they faced. This process had a number of major advantages, including – very important in terms of the perspective of this chapter – the crucial fact that we would work on issues which they owned, rather than working to some abstract statement of skills which all directors 'ought' to be able to deploy.

The significance of this sequence of analytical processes is heightened if the results are used not only to determine the content of the development programme, but actually to form the focus of real effort as well. While careful analysis of needs can ensure that the programme gets closer to performance requirements than an acceptance of some general statement of director skills, the most effective learning design would also employ the reality of directors' own performance requirements as the basis for real work as directors during the programme. For both participants and course tutors this kind of focus is – precisely because it is dealing with real issues – more interesting, more productive, but of course more risky.

To take one example, it would no doubt be common ground for anyone trying to deal with director-level needs that something on strategy would probably emerge as a strong element. If as a result of a careful analysis it did indeed emerge as one of the topics to be considered on a programme, it could be addressed through the usual variety of methods available in management education and training. There would be conceptual and theoretical inputs by a distinguished professor, by a highly paid consultant (two categories which are not mutually exclusive!), by the current exemplar of Chief Executive excellence. Books would be selected and made available – perhaps with appropriate chapters or pages indicated to reduce the burden of reading. In some organisations a series of case studies would be presented for analysis and discussion as a basis for interpreting and redefining participants' own experience of strategy. Directly or indirectly the existing strategy of the organisation would probably be reviewed through some such question as 'Review your own strategy against the inputs we have had so far on the programme; what aspects of it seem to you now to require further thought and/or change?'

Such a process, when well handled with serious attention and participation, can achieve quite a lot in terms of encouraging directors to reconsider their strategy. The main snag of such a method or collection of methods, however, is the familiar one of transfer. How do directors take back what they have learned through this exceptionally reflective experience, quite unlike their normal life as directors, into the often frantic reality of their working life? Everyone is by now only too familiar with the fact that at all sorts of levels managers and directors who have 'learned' some illuminating knowledge and perhaps developed some specific skills on a training programme find it difficult to apply their learning to their real work. (Note that I have presented the course in the most favourable light, where these teaching methods have actually been used with full relevance and well applied tutorial skills.)

The problem, really, is that for many years tutors have been seduced by an inappropriate teaching process, grounded in the acquisition of knowledge as the prime ambition rather than directed at the acquisition and deployment of skills. They have therefore constructed situations which are much more appropriate to the presentation (but rather less to the acquisition) of knowledge. Moreover, they have created a working environment in the classroom which is totally different both physically and psychologically from that in which managers and directors actually operate. They have created an unreality and asked managers to undertake the very difficult task of translating themselves from that unreality into their real world. We should not be surprised that many of them fail to make that transition.

It is far better, therefore, not only to work on the real issues faced by, in this case, directors but to use those real issues not simply as examples or goals but as the working content of the programme. So, to return to the example of 'strategy', the culmination of a view of using reality in order directly to impinge on performance is to ask people actually to work on their existing strategy, or to develop a new one. Moreover, the attempt to do this is conducted as the main feature of the exercise, not simply as a concluding illustrative aspect of a two-day course on strategy. The philosophy behind this approach is that a development programme aimed at performance skills is driven throughout by the identification of problems and opportunities, which then generate a demand for purposive development of skills and supporting knowledge. This is in contrast to the more traditional education and training view which presumes the knowledge and skills requirement and then tries to direct that knowledge towards the problem.

The difference of approach is crucially important in terms of our improved understanding of how managers and directors learn. They are, of course, primarily driven by task and performance requirements and not by abstract understanding of knowledge needs. A programme of the kind described in this case study, therefore, is not only practically more geared to presenting learning requirements through task and performance requirements, but also provides another major psychological and practical benefit. Working on real problems is again justified by the double value argument identified in the previous case. The problem with a great deal of management training and education is that it is difficult to evaluate and, in consequence, difficult to provide clear financial justification for it. All too often it has been presented and experienced as a matter of faith that it is valuable. If, instead, we work on the reality of performance requirements, the benefits are primarily felt in terms of precisely achieved performance – although, of course, it will be recognised that learning has been associated with that improved performance.

There are two features of these director programmes which remain to be described. In contrast with the Ford programme, they deal with a substantial variety of required skills, not with a relatively narrow though important particular problem of 'managing the matrix'. In addition to this issue of strategy used as an illustration, the director programmes have usually addressed five or six other major themes such as:

- The Job of a Director
- Directing Change
- The Board as a Team
- Achieving Success in Different Cultures
- Selecting and Developing Key Executives.

Priorities and resources may at any time require, as in the case of Ford, attention to an absolutely predominant managerial skill requirement. The potential difficulty, of course, is that heightened skill in one area is not supported by other requirements. It may become slightly out of proportion since a particularly important skill, however effectively developed, cannot contribute as much as it should to organisational performance when managers or directors lack other skills necessary to support total performance.

The second significant feature will already have been identified by some readers. In essence, the programme described is based on the principles of Action Learning. Indeed in each case the programme, in addition to the themes identified above, involved directors working on a major personal or board project or problem. Not only was this again important in terms of working on real performance issues, but from the point of view of the learning design for the programme, in most cases it represented a significant integrating factor, drawing together the various themes. It is sometimes forgotten in management education and training that managers rarely deal with totally discrete functional problems such as marketing or finance. They actually deal with problems involving a variety of functions, a variety of skills and a variety of competing requirements.

The third significant element is that the whole development programme must be geared through an understanding by the individuals of their own learning process, in relation to a programme which has been designed to help them with that process and also again has been designed according to the principles of the learning cycle.

The cases above illustrate the first strategy identified at the beginning of the chapter. Both these versions of performance-related skills training are driven not only by the needs of the organisation but by the line managers or personnel advisers within the organisation.

Organisation-Sponsored Individual Analysis

These two cases deal with common group needs and rather less with individual differences. The most structured and most obviously performance-related individual diagnosis is provided by Assessment Centres. When properly designed, it is based on a carefully produced and validated series of performance requirements for a variety of managerial jobs and uses an assessment process (again carefully validated) to enable individuals to be assessed and to assess themselves against those criteria. Then, again in the best managed development organisations, the development implications are worked on at the end of the process. (There are, of course, examples of a less happy situation where assessment remains the only purpose, with no development actions indicated or help provided.) Some Assessment Centres have indeed been converted by description and practice into Development Centres. Providing the performance criteria have been properly identified, the identification of needs will be strongly related to the management of performance. In well managed organisations and through well directed centres, this can again lead to the explicit provision of training to meet those performance requirements.

An alternative approach, not depending on previously validated performance standards, involves what is known as Individual Development Plans, Personal Learning Plans, Learning Contracts or Learning Agreements. Here the emphasis is still on identifying the performance needs of individuals, but it is tackled as the prime purpose of a discussion and subsequent plan rather than just an addendum to an appraisal process. Similar to the Assessment Centre or Development Centre approach in terms of its likely individuality and specificity, the difference is that the individual is treated throughout on an individual basis, never in a group. It is also, perhaps, less likely to draw on a previously identified list of performance criteria.

Opportunistic Strategies

So far we have looked at different versions of the structured and formalised approach to management development portrayed in my model of management development as Type 3.[4] However, as I argued in my book, if we pay attention in management development only to those highly structured, carefully identified development experiences, managed largely by personnel professionals, we are missing a large part of the reality of management development. Even in those organisations which manage their management development most effectively, most managers learn most from a variety of unplanned experiences, often untouched by any personnel professional hand. Entirely task-centred, these experiences are usually unplanned, and learning from them is in consequence relatively unconscious, although they may be recognised subsequently as major and significant learning experiences. What is needed is a process which increases the recognition and use of these opportunities as they occur.

Self-development as an Opportunistic Strategy

One of the causes of the self-development movement in the UK in the mid–1970s was the recognition that Management Development had been taken too much out of the hands of the manager, with responsibility placed inappropriately in the hands of personnel people. Management development had become something done 'to' managers rather than something done 'with' them. One of the main themes of the self-development process, therefore, has been to enable individuals to identify for themselves those aspects of their working and personal life within which they want to develop their knowledge, skills or attitudes. One result of this, supported by the values of many of the leaders of the self-development movement, has been the encouragement of an holistic approach – in which development is seen as concerned with the whole person rather than simply the job-centred and performance-related aspects which have been the concern of this chapter. The prime features of self-development are the combination of self-analysis (not organisational diagnosis), self-identification of needs, and identification of a range of learning opportunities both on and off the job.

The self-development process is certainly one which needs to be considered here, even though it embraces more than performance issues. In terms of analysing needs, there are of course great similarities with the formal assessment of needs generated through an appraisal. Just as in the better versions of appraisal schemes individuals will be asked to conduct self-assessment of their own performance and needs, so in the self-development mode they will similarly be asked to review themselves. The most familiar examples of this are contained in the book by Pedler and his colleagues.[5] Individuals may appraise themselves against a standard list such as that contained in Pedler's book, or against a list generated specifically for the organisation. Conceivably they may even start with a blank sheet and generate their own statements of performance criteria, how close they are to meeting them, and what they think should be done about meeting them. The actions, therefore, may include proposals for courses. One of the dangers here is that all too often the solution suggested is indeed a training course, rather than an attempt to discover a more effective answer through an on-the-job learning or development experience.

Courses Are Not the Only Answer

One major virtue of the newer ideas in this area is that the temptation to identify courses as the sole solution is reduced. The more sophisticated management development advisers now increasingly present in organisations have the capacity to help managers identify learning experiences *through* the job rather than necessarily resorting to formal training experiences. Three different approaches to satisfying the same performance need will help to illustrate the point:

Example 1
A manager is moved from a job in the organisation's Marketing Planning to one in the Supplies Department. The latter job involves a great deal of negotiation with suppliers, with the prospect of securing better terms in quality, delivery and price. The manager involved is given no formal training or guidance, and is expected to 'pick up' how to perform satisfactorily.

Example 2
A few years later another manager makes exactly the same move and is faced with the same issue of having to negotiate success-fully. By this time, however, previous difficulties have persuaded the organisation to take the problem more seriously. Instead of expecting the manager to learn on the job by some accidental, unreviewed, hit-and-miss method, a course on negotiation skills has been identified and the manager is placed on it within the first few weeks of joining the new department.

Example 3
In another division of the organisation a manager makes a very similar transition, again to a department involving negotiation skills. In this case, however, the department chooses to provide a planned learning experience through the job rather than through a course. The new manager has a carefully prepared development plan with specific learning objectives drawn up, one of which relates to the enhancement of negotiation skills. The plan identifies two different role models who can be observed by the new manager in action. In addition, learning review per-iods are built in as part of the induction period during which the observation of effective others is discussed and analysed. The manager is prepared for his or her first negotiation, which is then monitored by a more senior person.

Thus performance skills can be developed by a process other than off-the-job training in the traditional sense.

Integrating Performance and Development

This chapter makes the case that the enhancement of performance through training is most likely to be achieved when the training itself is focused on performing real tasks of significance to those involved. The second proposition is that such activities can be designed effectively through the adoption of the principles of learning which include the learning cycle and individual learning styles.[6]

The third proposition is that if we are concerned with performance skills, as distinct from knowledge or attitudes, it is necessary to enhance the relationships between – in fact to integrate – the different kinds of learning offered through course 'training' and by direct experience (which usually has the wider title of learning and development). The primary reason for this is that unless we attempt to achieve this, skills training will still be seen as an isolated event which, however brilliantly managed at the time, will cease to have a continuing impact on the manager as learner. If we want to make sense of the principles of continuous learning and development we must provide for continuity of thoughtfulness about both the managing process itself and the learning associated with it.

This means, as mentioned earlier, explicit attention to the learning process. It also means considered attention to that variety of learning opportunities which exist outside the brilliantly contrived learning experiences which so often spring to mind as the answer to performance-related skills requirements. This predicates attention not only to well designed, structured experiences of the kind illustrated in the case studies but to enabling individuals to continue to pay attention to their performance-related skills requirements through those many opportunities which exist within and around the job. This is the area in which least has been offered by formal management development processes, and in which, therefore, the greatest productivity improvements in management development terms are still available. The effective recognition and use of the wide variety of opportunities to learn on the job must complement the structured training experiences which have formed a large part of this chapter.

A Summarising Exercise

Since so much of this chapter has been concerned with the need to focus on real work, it seems desirable to give readers a piece of further work to do (I would not suggest that reading is an unreal activity!). Here is an exercise some might wish to undertake:

---

1 Have I, or has my organisation, undertaken any activities similar to those identified here?

2 If so, with what results?

3 Has this chapter indicated some areas worthy of investigation in terms of my choice of strategy for dealing with the development of performance management skills?

4 Which of the two strategies might be most successful in my organisation?

5 In what ways could I integrate off-the-job and on-the-job development of performance skills?

Figure 3.1 A Self-analysis Exercise

4

Appraisal

by Roger Holdsworth

Why Appraisal?

This chapter considers a number of questions about appraisal. How does it fit in with performance management, and with the subjects of the other chapters in this book? Why has appraisal always been a controversial issue? How have appraisal systems evolved and what are the current trends? What are the principal options for an organisation wishing to optimise its use of appraisal? What are the typical problems encountered in implementing appraisal, and how can we respond to them? What are the practical steps to be taken, in order to move forward towards an improvement in appraisal practices in the context of performance management?

Links with Performance Management

At the simplest level, one might even assert that performance management *is* appraisal – and vice versa. The cynic, on coming across Performance Management (with initial capitals) for the first time might, after requesting a definition of it, say 'Ah! I see – it's a new name for appraisal.' Conversely, performance management is a significant current focus of organisations' appraisal schemes.

Yet as performance management is an aspect of appraisal, so appraisal is part, and only part, of performance management. All the other chapters in this book relate to issues which are considered to be part of *their* province. How, after all, could one seriously attempt to discuss appraisal without touching on the measurement of performance and on the concept of rewarding people in relation to their performance? In the early days of appraisal history, these issues (discussed here in Chapters 2 and 5) were both the rationale and the stumbling block of many organisations' appraisal schemes. The link between appraisal and pay has always been a contentious issue. So too has the measurement of performance – the balance between quantitative and qualitative appraisal, between *post hoc* analysis and forward-looking development. As appraisal became more focused on the individual and on development, the burning issues centred on appraisal as a counselling process, on prescribing skills-improvement actions, and on the identification of potential, succession planning or career development (see Chapters 6, 3 and 7 respectively). And it has usually been recognised that the real crux of appraisal is not in the appraisal process itself, but in following it up, achieving the feedback loop so that the system really does serve the objectives of the organisation, the business, its teams and its individual members (see Chapters 8 and 1).

Is Appraisal Really Necessary?

Critical evaluation is at once a uniquely human capacity and a major preoccupation of the species. In this sense appraisal is a self-evident necessity – we cannot help appraising each other and even (sometimes) ourselves. But, if it is to this extent inescapable, why do organisations find it necessary to *require* their managers to appraise, and why did Anne Roe (1952) call her DSIR survey of appraisal schemes in British organisations *The Reluctant Appraiser*?

Appraisal is a compulsively fascinating subject, full of paradoxes and love-hate relationships. And appraisal schemes *are* really controversial. Companies carry out a major overhaul of their policies and practices in this area about every third year on average. Some schemes are popular, with overtones of evangelical fervour, while others are at least equally detested and derided as 'the annual rain dance', 'the end of term report', etc.

Those appraised are sometimes as reluctant as the appraisers. It is one thing to want feedback, another to relish negative criticism. Even worse, if the criticism is to be recorded in writing, shared with others, used in evidence against one. . . Often it is the formal and procedural aspects of appraisal which offend. Continuing, mutual communication relating to performance is universally regarded as a good thing. If only all managers (and subordinates) gave adequate time and effort to this on a monthly, weekly, even daily basis (in the manner advocated in Blanchard and Spencer's *One-Minute Manager*), would an appraisal *scheme* really be needed at all?

One of the paradoxes of appraisal schemes is that the managers who need them, in the sense that they would not give feedback to their subordinates *without* a mandatory scheme (probably with a form that has to be completed by a certain date), may be practically incapable of appraising objectively and constructively *within* the context of a scheme. The managers who appraise well, on the other hand, probably do not need to be told to do it this way, by this date and so on. We should be quite clear that appraisal schemes can be worse than useless, and even more certain that in individual cases the effect of an appraisal may be a worsening, not only of a working relationship, but of actual performance too.

On the other hand, the paradox *can* be reversed. No doubt the discipline of even an annual appraisal 'event' guarantees in many individual cases a minimum of formal attention to important issues, a chance for communication which would otherwise not take place. At the other end of the scale, many excellent natural appraisers (on a day-to-day basis) speak of the additional benefits of a periodic review, an opportunity to step back from the purely operational or incidental to look at performance and development in a broader and longer-term context.

Elements of an Appraisal System

Ask someone to describe their organisation's appraisal system, and the response is liable to be like this:

> Well, around February your manager sends you a form to prepare and suggests a date for your appraisal interview. After the interview the manager completes another form: you have an opportunity to see this, to add a comment of your own, and to sign it. Then one form is passed to the 'grandparent' (your manager's manager), before going on to the personnel department.

The point of this caricatured description is that it is entirely procedural, and a general criticism of appraisal practices is that they over-emphasise procedure. Of course, some procedures are more likely to help and others more likely to hinder, but choice of procedure should follow from the objectives of appraisal, and the success of an appraisal scheme is likely to depend less on procedure than on two other elements: skills and attitudes.

However good and sensible an appraisal scheme may seem on paper, the people who have to implement it have abundant scope to scuttle it if they resent it as an intrusion, or for some reason do not believe it will be useful to them. On the other hand, even theoretically poor schemes have been very successful when appraisers and appraisees have decided to work together to make them work, often adapting or bending the rules a little to achieve this. Consideration of attitudes is perhaps the single most important point to watch in setting up or modifying an appraisal scheme, and the last section of this chapter returns to it.

The skills of appraisal are no less fundamental. They are of three major types:

- *Structuring:* setting objectives and standards, data collection
- *Perceptiveness:* being a good and fair judge of performance, understanding individual differences
- *Communication and interaction:* using listening skills as well as the ability to share opinions in a constructive way.

Chapter 2, on performance measurement, has dealt with the structuring skills in some detail, and Chapter 6, on coaching and counselling, deals with interaction and communication. Note that the skills are required of the appraiser and appraisee alike. All too often appraisal has been seen as something a manager does 'to' a subordinate, rather than something they do *together*. Appraisal training has mainly been directed towards appraisers only.

Professor Gerry Randell, one of the authors of *Staff Appraisal*,[1] used to propose that organisations considering the introduction of an appraisal scheme should wait a couple of years, and concentrate first on developing the appraisal skills which would give a subsequent scheme at least half a chance of succeeding.

Why 'Appraisal'?

The word 'appraisal' has so far appeared 43 times in this chapter. Synonymous words and phrases have intentionally been avoided, but let us now consider for a moment 'what's in a name'.

In the early 1970s, a personnel director at British Steel briefed a consultant about to train senior managers in the relevant skills: 'At British Steel, we don't call it "appraisal". We find *that* a backward-looking word, dissecting the past, opening up old wounds and so on. We want our emphasis to be constructive, developmental, forward-looking. We prefer to call it – "assessment".' At about the same time, the Post Office called their process 'appraisement'. And so on.

To the average person in the street, 'appraisal' may mean little or nothing, whereas to the personnel specialist it has become *the* quasi-technical term for the subject of this chapter, so much so that this is the only chapter in the book with a single word title! 'Assessment' – in this context – would now more typically be associated with psychometric testing or 'assessment centre' programmes, both of which will be touched on in the section on appraisal options.

It is no doubt worth considering what to call a scheme, in order to emphasise both its purposes and its (participative) style. A medium sized consultancy recently re-named its scheme the 'Performance and Development Review'. Fine, but a bit of a mouthful, and everyone still refers to it as 'appraisal'!

Trends in Appraisal

Objectives of Schemes

Formalised staff appraisal probably started in the 1920s, and was predominantly a phenomenon of large, American corporations. Major objectives were to provide a basis for central decision-making (about pay and promotion, etc.) and to boost morale. These aims were found to be somewhat in conflict with each other, a theme which still persists. Clearly the type of appraisal scheme best suited to the former will not necessarily achieve the latter.

An American survey of 94 companies in the 1950s showed salary review and promotion decisions to be the two most quoted chief aims of appraisal. Performance improvement came only ninth in the popularity chart. The same survey, and many others which have followed, testified to the multiplicity of purposes to which appraisal can be put and for which it is instituted. Writers have often queried whether a single scheme can achieve such diverse aims: they advocate the choice of one or two major aims, but have sometimes omitted to say how the other purposes should be achieved.

British surveys as early as the late 1960s (BIM information summaries 133 and 136) showed that 'performance improvement' was already becoming the number one aim of companies' appraisal schemes, although often paired with the identification of training needs and long-term potential. Much more recently, Long noted a very definite emphasis on current rather than future performance.[2]

Over the past 15 years, the UK has seen two major developments in relation to appraisal and the identification of potential. One has been the realisation that conventional line manager appraisal does not achieve this particular aim at all well. The parallel development has been the meteoric rise of the 'assessment centre' to fill this need.

For many years the 'loser' in terms of appraisal aims was salary review. The linking of remuneration with appraisal went comprehensively out of fashion in the 1960s and 1970s. The main argument was that you cannot expect appraisees to be self-critical and examine their need to improve current job performance when next year's salary hangs in the balance. However, if an organisation wants to remunerate its employees on merit – or at least to include a strong performance element – then salary reviews must somehow be related to performance appraisal. If a separate appraisal rating is carried out as a basis for remuneration, surely appraisees should have an opportunity to discuss this with their manager? Are we not then back where we started from?

The most common 'solution' to this problem is to base salary reviews loosely on performance appraisal, and to separate the two events in time, perhaps by three months or so. Clearly this is more of a fudge than a solution, but it remains a very pervasive practice. On the other hand, more organisations are now attempting to grasp this nettle, and Chapter 5 on performance-related pay elaborates on this.

Evolution of Appraisal Styles

Appraisal is really an ongoing process, an important aspect of day-to-day relationships, chiefly between manager and subordinate. This is not just a desideratum, but also a statement of the inevitable. Even if we label a particular annual event 'appraisal', what happens in it will reflect what happens during the rest of the year. A directive manager can scarcely (and probably should not attempt to) become consultative for this one session, just because the Appraisal Manual stipulates (sic) the latter style.

Actual appraisal style (i.e. management style as manifested in appraisal events) is clearly very individual. But the average behaviour has undoubtedly evolved over the last four decades, and the following caricatured descriptions seem to apply.

In the beginning was the *Confidential Report*. 'The company has got to the size, Smithson, that one no longer knows all the staff, let alone their potential. Kindly let me have some notes on the people in your department. Nothing too formal or elaborate, just in your own words. No, I wouldn't let them know I've asked for this. It might make them uneasy, or it could raise expectations.'

Then came the *Character Assessment*. 'Your reports were very interesting, Smithson, but it was difficult to make comparisons across departments. Why don't we agree on some standard headings – let's say intelligence, common sense, leadership, co-operation, initiative and integrity – and give everyone marks out of 10, with five as average.'

This was followed by *Tell and Sell*. 'The numerical exercise was really revealing, but I was shocked to find how many people were getting less than seven out of 10 on several of the headings. Please arrange to have these people in for a chat – one at a time, of course. Let them know where they are going wrong, and give them some good advice about how to improve.' If this sounds exaggerated, remember that appraisal interviews in the 1960s were often *mandatory* only for appraisees whose ratings were below average!

Next was *Tell and Listen*. 'People often don't agree with their manager's appraisal of them. Sometimes they think that the problem lies more in the manager's behaviour than in their own. And they tend to resent what they see as personal criticism. So – give praise as well as negative criticism. Always start and end with positive encouragement [sometimes known as the 'personnel sandwich'!]. And make them really feel that you're listening to them, and prepared to take criticism yourself. Concentrate on objective behaviour (time-keeping, adherence to procedures, job knowledge and so on), rather than on sensitive aspects of character.'

Writers on appraisal were already advocating a *Joint Problem-Solving Approach*. 'Poor performance has to be treated as a shared problem. You have to work at it togther, and find a joint solution. As for criticism, appraisal should be like a "mutual confession of sins". And it has to be focused on previously agreed, quantifiable targets, in key result areas, although you need to look at underlying issues and qualitative aspects too. Make it the appraisee's session, get them to do most of the talking. Say "we" and "us" a good deal. Above all, be yourself and totally sincere.' Despite the satire here, and the fact that not everyone will have achieved the Nirvana of the joint problem-solving approach (proposed by Maier and others some 30 years ago), appraisal expectations and practice *have* evolved, in the four main ways summarised below.

Summary of Trends

Appraisals have become more *open*. The majority of current schemes formally require that the appraisee sees most if not all of the completed appraisal document. From a starting point of secrecy as a matter of policy, and subsequent criticisms of schemes resulting in 'character assassination', sharing of data gradually became the order of the day. Appraisees, of course, are not satisfied with being told the gist of their appraisal, hence the need for them actually to see and perhaps even sign the written document. In the 60s and 70s a usual compromise was for the appraisee to see the section of the form relating to job performance, with any assessment of promotion potential being kept secret. Shell was an early exception and a shining example of how constructive it could be to share the appraisal of an employee's 'ultimate level of promotability'.

The *purpose and content* of appraisal have changed, as already discussed. From pay and promotion to performance management and personal development, from character (only 20 years ago a major British retailer asked appraisers to assess 'moral courage' among other attributes) through more observable behaviour to key results. There probably was a phase when appraisal became depersonalised, the needs of the individual being lost in an overly task-oriented session which at worst was indistinguishable from a business review meeting. Performance management has to combine task-orientation with person-orientation.

The style has become more *dynamic*. Appraisal is now seen as being less about recording, more about changing and developing, and this entails a very active participation by the appraisee, initiating as much as possible of the process. Shared appraisal ratings tend to be more lenient than unshared ones. An American aircraft manufacturing company found that the average numerical rating leapt up a whole point (on a five-point scale) when they introduced open, as opposed to confidential, appraisal. In some people's view this implies that open appraisal tends to be insincere. On the other hand, it might be felt unethical to commit to writing any negative criticism which one is not prepared to make to someone's face. More fundamentally, many researchers in appraisal hold that negative criticism *per se* is counter-productive. Suggestions for improvement, to be useful, really need to come at least as much from the appraisee as from the appraiser, and emphasis on self-appraisal has grown considerably. A large management consultancy based the appraisal of their consultants on self-assessment, and claimed that their main problem was that the consultants tended to be overly self-critical.

Ownership of the appraisal has tended to shift from the centre to the periphery, from the personnel department to the manager and the appraiser. Appraisal involves a good deal of time and effort, and this will be given only if it is seen as a worthwhile investment. A cold storage firm had an appraisal scheme initiated by the personnel department, but the scheme was not a success, with only a small proportion of forms being properly completed and returned. Operations staff in the geographically dispersed cold stores resented having to give up time to this form-filling exercise on behalf of people in the 'ivory tower' headquarters with whom they had little contact. The scheme was then totally revised to become a process owned by manager and appraiser, who kept the only two copies of the appraisal summary (basically a record of agreed action). To ensure compliance, they did have to send a slip to the personnel department which said, in essence, 'We've done the appraisal, and we'll talk it over with you when next you care to visit us'! The revised scheme was a great success.

Appraisal Options

Types of Scheme

It will be clear already that appraisal schemes differ widely from each other. What appraisal means in one organisation might be quite unrecognisable under that name in another. While some appraisal practices are ineffective or even counter-productive, there is still a wide range of ways of appraising staff which have proved useful to particular companies. What are the main options?

We have already looked at the different possible objectives of appraisal, and to some extent the scheme will reflect the objectives which are particularly prioritised. We have looked at the concept of ownership and degree of centralisation of an appraisal scheme. The appropriate degree will depend both on the objectives and the degree of desirable bureaucracy in the organisation. Broadly, appraisal schemes occupy different positions on the following scales:

Procedurally orientated	Process-orientated
Orientated towards centralised decision making	Orientated towards local communication
Task- and performance-orientated	Person- and development-orientated
Highly structured appraisal documentation	Minimum of documentation
Formal link with salary review	Separate from salary review
Formal link with management development system	Development *per se*, but not formally linked to a system

Who Appraises Whom?

The current norm is for employees to be appraised by their immediate manager, but this is an over-simplification of the full situation. A few decades ago the immediate manager was thought to be rather too close to the appraisee to be entrusted with this process, and the manager's manager ('grandparent') often carried out the appraisal interview. It is still quite usual for the grandparent to play a role in 'signing-off' the appraisal, particularly in more procedurally orientated schemes. The manager's manager should bring a wider perspective to the process, and often benefits him/herself from involvement.

For a time it was thought that specialists (e.g. management development managers) could contribute to appraisal, as a catalyst or referee, but the logistics of such an involvement at the individual level (actually taking part in interviews) have generally proved prohibitive. More usually, management development staff will be involved in a review of appraisals, perhaps with the managers of a given division or function, sometimes as members of a management development committee with a balance of line and specialist expertise.

The open atmosphere which is advocated for appraisal implies that it should be a two-way process, including the appraisal of the boss by the subordinate. For several decades writers on appraisal have predicted that appraisal by subordinates would become a key feature, but this has not really occurred other than very exceptionally. How could it work? Would each subordinate do a separate appraisal and conduct a separate interview, or would it be a group affair? In one small plastics firm each manager was rated by their manager, by up to six peers and by all their direct subordinates. Consultants had to be called in to compile consensus reports for feedback to the appraisee manager, the results were extremely confusing and contentious, and the experiment was not repeated.

Often the direct manager is by no means the only person with a good overview of the appraisee's performance, and it is very desirable that the manager seeks other inputs to the appraisal, as a matter of general good practice. These other inputs could include not only senior managers, but peers and/or subordinates, perhaps even people external to the company. A few companies have even formalised this process, requiring the appraiser and appraisee to identify two or three 'referees' whom the appraiser should contact in preparing for the appraisal session.

Appraisal Documentation

In many people's minds 'appraisal' principally conjures up a printed form. An appraisal interview (or discussion) probably needs some documentation in order to have a lasting effect, rather than merely producing a 'warm feeling'. But the form on its own will achieve very little.

The main purpose of an appraisal form is to record, for the benefit of appraiser and appraisee (and perhaps for some other third parties) the main conclusions of the appraisal session, in particular any agreed action plan, and probably also the data which led to the conclusions. The structure of the form may also guide the appraiser and help to ensure that the appraisal process follows a logical sequence of steps.

An open-ended appraisal form could consist of a number of questions with large boxes to be filled in, such as

What are the key objectives of this person's job, and how have they changed during the year?
What have been the significant achievements and failures?
What aspects of the job give most satisfaction and what are the main problems or irritants?
What should be the key job and personal performance objectives for next year?
How can we work together more effectively to improve performance?
How does this job fit into the appraisee's broader career and life perspective?

What action should be taken to develop the appraisee in this broader context?

These seven questions (or a similar set, depending on the appraisal scheme's objectives) could be all that was needed for a 'locally owned', process-orientated appraisal. But if the scheme is more oriented towards centralised decision making, it may seem necessary to structure the output more tightly in the interests of comparability, to make it more of a multiple choice rating form. This is where the fun, or more likely the pain and trouble, starts. The problems of rating are discussed in the next main section.

The appraisal form is not necessarily the only piece of appraisal documentation. Many companies have separate forms for appraisee and/or appraiser preparation, although probably the appraisal form itself, with an appropriate set of instructions, can serve this purpose. A manual or set of guidelines on appraisal is desirable and worthwhile. Appraisers (and appraisees) also need to have other supporting documentation at hand when preparing or implementing the appraisal, e.g. job description, last year's appraisal, diary, performance statistics, memoranda exchanged during the year, data on training undertaken.

Assessment Centres

About 30 years ago, a movement started in the USA which was really founded on the premise that the assessment of career potential cannot rest entirely on conventional performance appraisal. Rather, it needs to be supplemented by a more analytic observation of appraisees performing in standardised situations which simulate tasks and contexts relevant to future requirements.

The term 'assessment centre' is not particularly helpful. It is said to originate from the name given to the building which AT&T (the proponent par excellence of this method) dedicated entirely to such activity, with every manager within a certain category undergoing *annually* a programme of simulations. Hardly any other organisation has been as thorough as AT&T in this respect, but the movement has had considerable impact, chiefly in the USA and the UK, and it is estimated that nearly half of all UK companies with more than 1,000 employees use the assessment centre method at some level or other.

Essentially, assessment centres involve:

- *multiple methods:* various simulations (group exercises, in-tray exercises, presentations) and often also psychometric methods (personality questionnaires, occupational tests), each element being designed to assess specific competencies;
- *multiple assessors:* subjectivity is reduced not only by using more objective techniques but also by entrusting the assessment to a team, including both specialists (personnel/training/management development, perhaps even external consultants/psychologists) and line managers;
- *multiple candidates:* an assessment centre typically involves six or 12 candidates at a time, enabling their interaction to become part of the assessment material;
- *multiple dimensions:* assessment will be against a number (typically 10–12) of pre-defined dimensions, so that each candidate/participant emerges with a profile of scores and descriptions rather than (or as well as) an overall rating of potential;
- *multiple purposes:* the system is seen to work best when the aims are defined so as to balance assessment with development, the needs of the organisation with those of individual participants.

There is very well documented evidence that assessment centres are better at identifying potential than appraisal schemes. However, the assessment centre is invariably seen as a complement rather than an alternative to appraisal. The best assessment comes from combining both sources of data, and the assessment centre will be successful only if the conclusions from it are fed back into the performance appraisal process, usually by means of a three-cornered session between appraisee, line manager and an assessor from the assessment centre team.

Problems in Appraisal

Rejection

The central issue in appraisal is whether the intended population of appraisers and appraisees really take the process on board, and whether they will work together towards the aims of the scheme and develop the necessary skills to get the most out of it. Many appraisal schemes simply do not work, and are either abandoned or ignored. The final section of this chapter will address this issue and consider how to introduce/review a scheme so as to gain acceptance. Before that, some classic problems in the functioning of appraisal are reviewed.

Subjectivity

Many studies have testified to subjectivity as a significant problem. This has been demonstrated at a scientific level: different appraisers *do* come to different conclusions based on the same data, because they have different values, different likes and dislikes. This is also a problem at the individual, human level. Appraisees often consider their manager's assessment of them to be unfair, even biased, and this may render the whole process ineffective because of the perceived injustice.

Subjectivity can be reduced (but clearly not eliminated) by defining an appraisal process which concentrates on factual achievement rather than on style or character, by basing assessment on agreed objectives, by involving other 'referees' (see above) in the preparation stage, by making the appraisal interview itself an open, two-way process and inviting the appraisee to contribute a self-appraisal.

Central Tendency, Leniency/Severity

Particularly when numerical ratings are used, it has been observed that appraisers avoid giving extreme marks or opinions, tending to 'water down' their assessment; this is known as 'central tendency'. Its cause seems to lie partly in appraisers lacking confidence and failing to exercise sufficient discrimination, and partly in the communication process: appraisers do not like to give extreme signals. One study of appraisal ratings carried out in the 1970s by the author with the University of Nottingham and the National Computing Centre, examining the validation of graduate selection procedures, showed this distribution of assessments given:

Outstanding	6%
Very good	63%
Good	31%
Just acceptable	0%
Unsatisfactory	0%.

The population involved in this example was graduate entrants (appraised after two years in the company) and was supposed to include a good number of 'high fliers'. Why then were only 6% rated outstanding? Many appraisers avoid giving a top mark for fear that it will induce complacency, while some admit that a top-rated subordinate can constitute a threat to the appraiser him/herself!

The above distribution, typical not only for recent graduates but for any appraisee group, also shows the problem of leniency. On the whole, appraisers err in the direction of pulling their punches, not confronting appraisees sufficiently with their short-comings. One corporation, involved in large-scale executive redundancies during the early 1980s, found it was often having to tell people who had been rated 'good' for many years that they were really under-performers.

Appraisers are lenient to different degrees, and some (though exceptions) are better described as severe. Different 'norms' used by different managers obviously pose an acute problem when ratings have to be compared (for salary or promotion purposes, for instance).

The use of a senior manager ('grandparent' or other) as a moderator of appraisals can reduce the problem of different norms. Great ingenuity has been shown in proposing solutions to the general problems of leniency and the central tendency, and many theses written on the advantage of scales with an even (or odd) number of scale points. 'Behaviourally anchored rating scales', with descriptions of typical behaviour at various anchor points, had a great vogue and do help to an extent.

Halo, Recency and Contrast Effects

A persistent problem in all assessment has been called the 'halo effect'. This is the tendency to rate someone with, say, one particular quality as being *generally* good – hence the halo. Obviously the reverse can happen too, so that an unfortunate subordinate with one marked (or even supposed) weakness can get written off as being generally useless or lacking in potential. To some extent, managers can be trained to be more analytic, and the appraisal form or process can be designed to help them be less generalising. Use of the assessment centre technique as a supplement to appraisal ensures that the halo effect (or 'norms' effect at the other end of the scale) is reduced.

Appraisers are prone to put too much emphasis on the most *recent* behaviour or impression – 'You are only as good as your last week's figures' is a saying common among branch managers in some building societies – instead of judging the whole period to be covered by the appraisal.

There are also various types of *contrast* effect in assessment. The one that occurs most markedly in performance appraisal is often allied to recency. If a normally well-rated individual performs slightly less well than would be expected of them, this can come out as an exaggeratedly low performance rating, an utter fall from grace. Conversely, a fairly average bit of performance from someone who is usually considered weak can get out of proportion. The problems of the recency and contrast effects respond to some degree to training.

Appraisal: What To Do

An organisation intending to set up or overhaul an appraisal scheme, in the context of performance management, should consider following the process shown below:

1 *Set up a Working Group*
   Commitment to the (new) scheme is vital. It must be seen as being for, and belonging to, the population group intended. Whereas the personnel/management development function should be involved, they should from the outset work with other functions. The working group (probably six to eight people) should be representative vertically as well as horizontally.

2 *Define the Objectives*
   Be precise as to the outcomes wished for. Do not just say that performance improvement is desired, but state how it will be measured. How will the scheme link with pay, and how with personal development? How will it relate to other existing procedures, e.g. to assessment centres?

3 *Design Methods and Procedure*
   Be creative in thinking about how best the objectives can be met. Who will be asked to appraise whom, when and how?

4 *Draft Documentation*
   Keep things as simple as possible, but still be reasonably explicit. Who is going to have access to the documentation? Can appraisees use the same form as appraisers for their preparation?

5 *Communication*
   Although communication is vital at the stage when draft documentation of the scheme is available, this is far too late to

start communicating about it. There is a risk that the consultative spirit implicit in setting up the working group (step 1) stops there, that this group becomes the 'in group' and keeps information and ideas to itself. What is needed instead is frequent, broad communication, at all levels, and using a variety of methods: written communication certainly, but backed up by meetings. And this communication should be two-way. Meetings can be used to test ideas, along with surveys (by interview and questionnaire) to improve the fit between the ultimate scheme, its purpose and its context, and to sell it in depth.

6 *Pilot Project*
It is advisable to pilot the scheme in one smallish department, division or other group, for various reasons. A pilot project can be a useful communication and participation device. It also enables the working group to modify some aspects, without loss of credibility, as a result of experience from the pilot. Remember that the introduction of an appraisal scheme is quite a high-risk enterprise. The group to choose for the pilot should be one which will act as an effective ambassador for it.

7 *Training*
Everyone involved in appraisal needs training in order to derive maximum benefit from the scheme. Because the scheme will presumably cover a number of tiers of management, many people will be involved both as appraisers and as appraisees. Of course, to maintain credibility, the scheme should in theory go right up to the top, but there can be legitimate questions about who appraises the chief executive. At the 'bottom end', there will be a tier of people who are involved only as appraisees, but they too should receive training. Training in appraisal can include briefing on the aims and procedures, but active participative discussion is also needed in order to influence attitudes. Skills training is invaluable, with case studies to increase awareness of problems such as the halo effect and central tendency, and role-playing interviews for development and increased self-awareness of appraisal style, typically using CCTV playback.

8 *Full Implementation*
The timetable for implementation requires careful thought. During the first cycle, additional specialist resources may be

needed to monitor progress and iron out problems as they arise. The timing planned for subsequent years may not be ideal for the first full run-through.

9 *Individual Follow-up*
Particularly during the first year's implementation, but also subsequently, sufficient resources have to be put aside for making sure that the scheme is working at the individual level, and that action plans are being put into action.

10 *Validation*
Validation is also necessary at an organisational level. Did the working group get it right first time? What further improvements could be made? It has been argued that an appraisal scheme needs some significant injection of new thinking at least every third year to keep it alive and dynamic. Continue to rely on participation and communication, and make selective use of surveys, briefings and meetings about how it is going and how it can be made to work better.

5

Performance-related Pay

by Vicky Wright

'He is well paid that is well satisfied;
And I, delivering you am satisfied,
And therein do account myself well paid:
My mind was never yet more mercenary
– Portia in *The Merchant of Venice*

Performance-related pay is probably the most controversial element of performance management. Many human resource managers, and their line colleagues, feel profoundly uncomfortable about linking pay to performance; several unions (such as the Banking and Finance Union) have policies that oppose it. But for every person who believes that performance-related pay cannot be part of an equitable, fair and effective reward system there is at least one who believes that without it no organisation can hope to construct a reward system appropriate to the turbulent, competitive world of today.

However, even the most ardent supporters of performance-related pay recognise that it is extraordinarily difficult to manage well. Most organisations which have performance-related pay arrangements are still trying to perfect this element of performance management; it is a part of managing people which requires constant attention and improvement.

But if performance-related pay is so difficult, why has it been taken out of the 'too difficult drawer' of so many organisations in the last few years? The answer simply is: pressure on performance has increased, the impact of individuals on success has increased and people have become a valuable, scarce and costly resource.

The economics of the situation are clear in many firms. For the average manufacturing company, the payroll constitutes about 40% of total costs; in service organisations, the proportion is often higher. In parts of the public sector, such as the Health Service, the payroll can make up over 75% of total costs. In these circumstances varying pay in line with performance can have major economic value to the organisation.

But the case does not rest on economics alone; there are strong reasons of human resource management. Individuals are becoming sophisticated in their relationships with their employers, and are often seeking better rewards based on their contribution. Readily accessible information and increased job mobility have heightened awareness of employment alternatives. Higher performers know their value elsewhere. With reduced promotion opportunities (the traditional reward for performance offered by many employers) and active labour markets, performance-related pay may be the only option for employers wanting to hold on to high performers.

Although some employers may feel forced into performance-related pay, there is also a strong positive case for it. In the current business environment performance-related pay, whether in the form of incentives (pre-agreed payments for certain levels of performance) or rewards (payments for performance achieved), is frequently used to support a performance-oriented 'culture'. If people are in organisations where managers are adopting styles which are strongly achievement-oriented, what can be the justification if one of the most potent communicators of values in the organisation is not in accord with all other communications?

There is also evidence that in performance-oriented cultures performance-related pay is seen by employees as a more equitable reward system than systems that offer no relationship to performance. At the individual level employee attitude surveys consistently show a preference towards performance-related pay; there is also evidence of a common expectation that when organisations are performing well employees should be able to share in that success. But if this is used as evidence it must be acknowledged that this shows only half the story. The reality of performance-related pay often does not live up to expectations. Many employees support performance-related pay expecting their pay will be higher as a result. This can be reinforced by lax performance appraisal. For example, a financial services company conducted a survey of its managerial population recently which showed over 75% in favour of a greater element of performance-related pay, but closer inspection also revealed that over 70% were appraised as superior performers.

Similarly line managers, often the strongest advocates of performance-related pay, frequently consider the advantages of

higher rewards for higher performers, rather than the implications of having to manage less pay for lower performers.

Performance-related pay brings with it some powerful, and
sometimes unpalatable messages to employees. The 'edge' that
performance-related pay gives, whether it is in the form of indi-
vidual-, team- or organisation-based incentives and rewards, has
to be managed. For example, the major retail banks in Britain
run profit-sharing schemes which have a large element of discretion in relation to payment levels. Although these have fluctuated
over the years, payments have seldom dropped below 5% of
salary. In 1991 all the banks recorded poor results due to serious
trading conditions in the UK. Lower profit shares and below-
inflation salary rises resulted in a total remuneration statement
showing total rewards lower in 1990/1991 than 1989/1990: a salu-
tary lesson in performance-related pay that came as a surprise to
many employees used to seeing pay always rising.

We also know that there are many organisations still struggling
for success in performance-related pay. In a survey conducted
by Wyatt[1] 58% of personnel managers said that performance-
related pay was ineffective in their organisations. By contrast
67% of personnel managers responding to the IPM pilot survey
of performance management in high-performing organisations[2]
said they believed that their performance-related pay arrangements supported improved performance.

In this difficult field the purpose of this chapter is not to fuel
the controversy; it seeks rather to provide an overview of good
practice and some practical advice on introducing and maintaining sound performance-related pay arrangements.

A Definition

'Performance-related pay' is a term used to cover a variety of
reward arrangements. Within organisations performance-related
pay (or its abbreviation 'PRP') can be used to designate a particular scheme – for example, the merit pay or bonus system. For
the purposes of this chapter the definition used it as follows:

> Performance-related pay is that part of the financial, or financially
> measurable, reward to an individual which is linked directly to
> individual, team or company performance.

The principal types of performance-related pay are merit pay,
individual incentive bonuses, individual discretionary bonuses,

team/company performance bonuses, skills-based payments and any other payments which employees may earn or receive related to individual, team or organisation performance improvement. This definition also includes performance-related arrangements that pay out in shares or gifts. Excluded from consideration are those payments which are made in the form of bonuses but are not performance-related, for example Christmas bonuses.

Why Do It?

Pay is one of the strongest communicators of how much an organisation values the contribution of an individual or group, but many people put a high test on performance-related pay. Does it actually motivate people? Does it lead to higher levels of individual and corporate performance?

There is no research which conclusively shows that there is a causal link between the presence of performance-related pay and high levels of organisational performance. But motivation is a field of academic study where theory abounds. It is not the purpose of this book to dwell on motivation theory in detail; however, for those who believe strongly in the motivational effects of performance-related pay the most commonly quoted model is *expectancy theory*. A simple diagram showing the main elements of this theory is shown in Figure 5.1.

As this model suggests, expectancy theory is not a simple 'carrot and stick' approach (people are more complex than the proverbial donkey). It indicates that pay is only a small part of a complex system – in particular, due account must be given to individual *perceptions* of reward, and the balance of intrinsic and extrinsic rewards. For example, those managers in the National Health Service who are currently being given greater freedoms in personnel management, including local determination of some aspects of pay, are finding that performance-related pay is part of a long list of possible actions to improve human resource performance. But it is not usually top of the list. Better job design, greater employee involvement, mobilisation of employee interest in quality of service, development of new competencies and benefits that will make life easier to staff used to working irregular hours are initiatives that will have an equal, if not greater impact on motivation. In summary, what the expectancy theory model tells us is that performance-related pay can play a part, but it is unlikely to be the sole means of gaining improved performance.

In practice, organisations that introduce performance-related

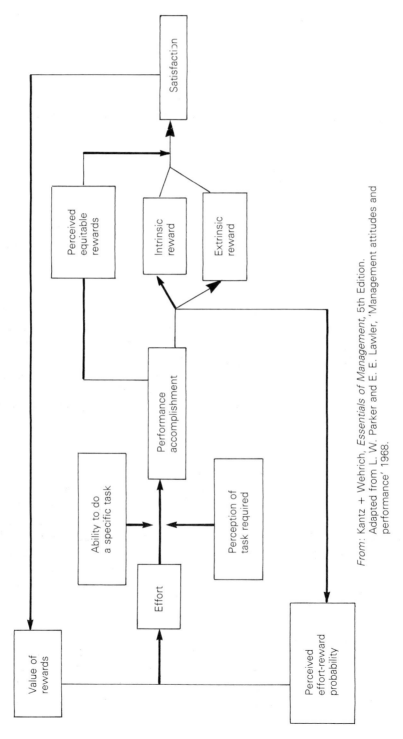

From: Kantz + Wehrich, *Essentials of Management*, 5th Edition.
Adapted from L. W. Parker and E. E. Lawler, 'Management attitudes and performance' 1968.

Figure 5.1: Expectancy Theory – A Model of Motivation

pay do so for a number of reasons. The most commonly quoted are:

Focusing Attention and Harnessing Effort Where the Organisation Wants It
There is research evidence[3] that many executive bonus schemes are successful in achieving a focus on those elements of performance that are measured in a bonus scheme.

Supporting a Performance-Oriented Culture
Bonus schemes and merit-only base salary pay reviews, linked to objectives-driven performance review, give clear messages to individuals that rewards are for contributions, not for just 'being there'. Organisations such as Dixons and Hanson have clearly communicated philosophies about reward linked to their management styles.

Emphasising Individual Performance or Teamwork as Appropriate
The trend towards individual managerial accountability has been matched by the development of individual bonuses. However, one of the downsides of executive and senior management bonus schemes identified in the mid–1980s[4] was the over-focus of some schemes on individual rather than team performance. This is now being rectified in many organisations (for example BP) by encouraging use of team bonuses where it is quite clear that team working is required to achieve high, and enduring, levels of performance.

Strengthening the Performance-Planning Process
Many organisations have difficulty in getting line managers to invest sufficient time and energy in performance management processes. Introducing performance-related pay adds an 'edge' that normally ensures that performance appraisals are completed. For example, ICL, when they first introduced performance-related pay, rapidly increased the percentage of performance appraisals carried out to 100%; from this base it was then possible to invest in improving the quality of the appraisal process.

Rewarding the Right People
Many traditional organisations have operated semi-automatic incremental systems which have rewarded time in post rather than performance. As the pace of change and the pressure to perform in organisations have increased, the weighting given to

time in post, as opposed to contribution, has reduced. The right people to reward are now seen as those who are performing.

Motivating All of the People
Automatic increments to the top of a range normally come to an end if an individual stays in post for a significant length of time; organisations see performance-related pay as a way of keeping up the potential rewards for the high performers. In this respect performance-related pay, if well managed and designed, can support the motivation of all the people.

Sharing in Success and Increasing Employee Identification with the Business
Profit sharing and other 'corporate success sharing' schemes do not have a major or direct impact on employee behaviour.[5] Nonetheless many organisations regard these schemes as a useful support to other programmes which encourage employees to have a closer interest in the performance of the business.

The reasons outlined above are the most commonly mentioned by employers looking to introduce performance-related pay for the first time, but for those organisations that have had performance-related pay for several years they may seem rather stilted or contrived. In many organisations performance-related pay is now seen as the normal 'way we do things round here'; it is part of the culture. Performance-related pay is just the most appropriate way to structure reward.

Social psychologists have devoted considerable energy to studying the values people hold in relation to the distribution of pay, and performance emerges frequently as a main determinant in Western Europe and America. In a study conducted by John Fossum from the University of Minnesota,[6] three groups were involved in making hypothetical decisions about pay increases: college students, line managers and compensation managers. All three groups agreed that by far the largest consideration should be given to performance – ranking this higher than other plausible criteria such as cost of living, difficulty in replacing someone who leaves, seniority and organisational budget restraints. Similarly, employee attitude surveys in the UK frequently show a bias towards performance rewards, with civil servants as likely to support the concept as bankers, manufacturing line managers, clerical staff and employees on the shop floor.

So why is performance-related pay seemingly required to pass a higher test of fairness and robustness than seniority, automatic incremental systems and market pay rates? The answer appears to be that many organisations have not got performance-related pay systems already in place and that to introduce them disturbs existing systems which, however inadequate, are understood and operated with fewer difficulties and demands on line managers. But this is hardly an adequate response for dealing with the competitive environment of the 1990s; although there have been a few cases of organisations removing performance-related pay systems once introduced (e.g. one district council in the Midlands), the main direction seems to be *towards* performance-related pay as a fair base for reward.

The Pitfalls and Cautions

If the argument for introducing performance-related pay sounds compelling, those who operate such arrangements know that the gap between the promise of theory and the reality of what can be achieved is often very large indeed. The most obvious pitfalls are:

Inadequate Performance Management Systems
Many performance-related pay systems are not backed up by a high-quality performance management system. If performance management is not working, and not trusted by employees, then pay arrangements that depend on it are not going to be regarded as fair.

Too Much Focus on the Financial and the Quantifiable
Performance-related pay often leads to a focus on the hard measurable elements of performance rather than those elements of performance that are only assessable. This can lead to bureaucracy, a 'cottage industry' of financial measurement and, in some cases, a refocusing of effort on the things that are not necessarily at the heart of a job or role. While it is useful to have performance reward linked to the measurable and the meaningful, there are a number of jobs where the measurable is not meaningful, and the meaningful is not measurable.

Divisive Schemes
Most medium-size and large organisations are no longer controlled bureaucracies with simple production processes. Nonetheless, the designers of many performance-related pay schemes do not take sufficient account of the increasing importance of team

working, nor the inter-relationships between departments. For example, in a survey by Hay Management Consultants in 1988,[7] the most frequent criticism of executive bonus schemes was that they encouraged divisive, or competitive, behaviours in the top team.

Short Terminism and Inflexibility

The focus of many schemes has been criticised for being far too heavily biased towards the short term, with little emphasis on longer-term measures of performance, or support for innovations and investments which have delayed paybacks. Similarly, many schemes are not flexible enough to reflect changes in job demands that emerge during the year (for example, coping with an unexpectedly deep recession in 1991). This is a problem of performance management as much as of pay.

Costs

Like most changes to payment systems, the introduction of performance-related pay can cost money. This can result in substantially increased costs. If performance-related pay forms part of base salary, drift of 1 or 2% is not unusual. Bonus schemes introduced on top can result in additional costs of anything from nothing to 50% or more. The question here is whether the costs are under control, properly planned and justified on a cost benefit basis.

Corruption of the Performance Appraisal Process

It is *inevitable* that performance-related pay will have an impact on performance appraisal; the pitfall is not making allowances for it at the time schemes are introduced and taking action to avoid obvious problems.

Expecting Too Much

Unlike personnel interventions such as improved management development programmes or succession planning, many managers seem to expect that performance-related pay will sort out countless problems. Some that it won't are:

- poor performance management
- uncompetitive base salary policies
- deficient company performance
- functional pay problems
- poor management of people.

Forms of Performance-Related Pay

Performance-related pay can take a wide variety of forms; there is no such thing as an average or normal package. Figure 5.2 shows the main types organised by their principal performance focus (individual, team, corporate and mixed) and their time focus (short-term, longer-term and mixed).

		TIME FOCUS		
		SHORT-TERM (a year or less)	LONGER-TERM	MIXED
PERFORMANCE FOCUS	INDIVIDUAL	○ Individual bonus	○ Individual long-term cash incentives	○ Deferred individual bonuses
		○ Incentive gifts	○ Merit pay	
	TEAM	○ Team bonus	○ Team long-term cash incentive	○ Deferred team bonuses
			○ Performance unit plans	
	CORPORATE	○ Profit-sharing (or corporate success) bonus	○ Corporate long-term cash incentive	○ Deferred corporate bonuses
			○ 'Automatic' share options	
			○ Phantom options	
			○ Co-investment plans	
			○ Restricted stock	
	MIXED	○ Bonus based on multi-level performance criteria	○ Long-term cash incentive using multi-level performance criteria	○ Share options individually performance-related on grant
		○ Individual bonus from bonus pool		○ Individually geared performance unit plans

Figure 5.2 The Varieties of Performance-Related Pay

The most frequently used types of performance-related pay are outlined in this chapter. They are:

Merit pay
Individual bonuses
Team bonuses
Company-wide schemes
Share schemes
Incentive gifts
Skills-based pay.

Merit Pay

Merit pay is the most widespread form of performance-related pay, particularly for the growing 'white collar' labour force and must be familiar to all by now. It is that part of the base salary increase which is determined by reference to individual performance alone. An increasing number of organisations use merit as the sole determinant of pay rises to individuals, although for the majority in the UK general, or 'cost of living,' increases form the basic increase on to which merit pay is added. In 1990 Hay Management Consultants' Industrial and Service Sector pay survey showed that for managerial and white collar jobs 60% of companies now used 'merit only' pay increases and a further 18% had an element of the base salary increase linked to merit or performance. Although it is most commonly found in white collar jobs, merit pay is not unknown in production and shop floor environments.[8] Nissan is probably the best known employer using merit pay from top to bottom in the organisation.

Merit pay has a long track record as a form of performance-related pay, and many believe that, well managed, it is highly motivational. However, criticism of merit pay has been growing in recent years. Because it results in increases to base salary, merit pay can result in an upward drift in fixed payroll costs unless there is steady labour turnover. Concern about costs has led some organisations to impose strict control over merit budgets, but the lack of a sufficient pool of money to apply to merit pay and too little discrimination in the distribution can reduce its impact as an incentive. In these circumstances, merit pay can easily be overshadowed by general pay increases (particularly at times of high inflation) or payments from other performance pay schemes.

Merit pay has also been widely abused in order to deal with

other pay problems. Functional or market premia have often been hidden within the merit pay budget. If merit pay is to be successful in the future, organisations need to manage schemes better as well as finance them correctly.

Merit Pay Architecture

It is easy to fall into the trap of viewing merit pay as the easiest and least innovative first step in introducing performance-related pay. In the normal course of events base salary increases are awarded (or considered) in any case and it is therefore not really a new form of pay, just a different way of delivering what is familiar.

In practice, it is probably one of the most difficult performance-related pay programmes to operate successfully. Designing a merit or individual pay regime involves addressing a number of key practical questions such as:

- Do you establish pay matrices and pay ranges to determine pay increases and pay levels?
- How large a variation in pay do you want between high and poor performers?
- Do you make the link between performance rating and pay explicit?
- How to you involve line managers?

Pay ranges and their operation

Although by no means universal, most organisations with merit pay arrangements have pay ranges for individual jobs or grades, or operate pay spines over grade ranges. These ranges define the normal, upper and lower limits for individual pay. In some organisations the range between top and bottom is very significant (for example, the top may be double the bottom); in others the top may be only 20% more. The influences on choice are:

	Broad ranges	Narrow ranges
Pros	• Enable real differentiation on performance grounds	• Easy to control cost
	• Likely to have fewer problems recruiting within the range	• Can be used easily with other forms of performance-related pay
Cons	• More difficult to control costs	• Do not allow significant differentiation

On average, organisations find that pay ranges where the top is 1.5 times greater than the bottom gives a reasonable balance between control and flexibility.

Having established a range, the next question to address is the positioning of individuals and the method by which they progress within the range. There are two principal options:

a) *Incremental Systems* In this approach ranges or pay spines are divided into levels; higher performers progress faster through the range by skipping some of the levels, i.e. by being given additional increments. This approach is fairly simple to manage but suffers from the problem that eventually people reach the top of the range and continued high performance is no longer rewarded.

Some incremental systems prevent average performers from progressing to the very top of the range by operating performance bars at certain incremental points. Although a popular system for operating merit pay, there is a danger of decay, with automatic increments rewarding, in effect, length of service and not performance.

Incremental systems are common in the public sector (for example, the Civil Service and Kent County Council) and also in some large private-sector organisations (such as some of the major retail banks).

b) *Pay Matrices* An example of a pay matrix is shown in Figure 5.3. This assists in determining a new pay level for an individual by reference to his or her existing position in a range and the percentage increase to be awarded by reference to performance ratings. So, using this example, if an individual

POSITION IN RANGE

PERFORMANCE ASSESSMENT	80%–88%	89%–96%	97%–104%	105%–112%	113%–120%
OUTSTANDING 1	18%	15%	13%	11%	9%
SUPERIOR 2	15%	13%	11%	9%	8%
FULLY ACCEPTABLE 3	12%	10%	9%	8%	7%
INCOMPLETE 4	8%	5%	4%	0%	0%
MARGINAL 5	0%	0%	0%	0%	0%

Note: The figures used in each box of the matrix are for illustrative purposes only, to demonstrate the principles of how the matrix would work. In this example a market movement of 9% has been assumed.

Figure 5.3 Sample Salary Increase Matrix

is currently paid at the 90% point in the range and assessed as superior, the pay increase awarded is 13%. This method of managing merit pay avoids the rigidity of incremental points, but can itself become inflexible because of the mechanistic link between appraisal rating and the increases awarded. Several organisations using this approach find it economically inflationary if the performance appraisal arrangements are subject to 'rating inflation'. In trying to contain this, forced distribution of ratings is used in some organisations, but, given the well known disadvantages of such straitjackets, most organisations are seeking to minimise this problem through better management of the rating process and/or allocation of budgets to line managers, to give greater responsibility for management of pay.

Nonetheless, there are also other forces disrupting the smooth running of performance matrices which challenge the assumptions of the methodology:

i) Should outstanding performers take some time to reach the 100% point within the range? If this midpoint is pitched at the market rate, what justifies paying a high performer less than the full rate for the job?

ii) Is it right that higher performers in the higher part of the range get a lesser pay increase than a fully acceptable performer lower in the range?

iii) Should incomplete performance attract an increase at all?

This method of systematising merit pay was designed at a time when the prevailing value system still gave some weight to 'time in the job' and when it was generally possible to recruit and promote people to lower points in the range. Although pay matrices are still in widespread use, organisations which operate in very competitive labour markets and with a high internal commitment to performance often report that matrices are too conservative. They can be designed to have higher gearing, but even this can be inadequate to meet the culture and value demands in some organisations. In response to the perceived inadequacies of structured approaches to merit pay some organisations have attempted to remove or open up pay ranges significantly, and have less disciplined approaches to pay increases.

Pay ranges, incremental systems and merit matrices are not inevitable consequences of merit pay. Several well known organisations have managed merit pay systems without formal arrangements for several years, for example the John Lewis Partnership and Marks and Spencer in the retail sector. The underpinning for success in this approach is undoubtedly a high level of discipline in performance management and payroll cost management.

Is Merit Pay a Strong Performance Reward?

Merit pay is often rejected by the purists as open to abuse, not clear enough, bundling together too many aspects of performance, too seniority-related, a cost with insufficient benefits. Personnel managers themselves are often sceptics.

However, this form of performance-related pay shows no sign of disappearing; done well it seems to gain some influential supporters.[9] In practice, the operation of merit should, and often does, result in base salaries which are not only felt fair but represent (as far as this is possible to establish) the accumulated value of the individual in a particular job to the organisation. The challenge appears to be to keep such arrangements under strict cost control, and to keep the performance management arrangements up to the standard required to make this a strong performance reward.

Individual Bonuses

Individual performance or incentive bonuses are separately identifiable cash sums paid on the basis of individual performance, but not consolidated into base pay. This form of performance-related pay has most commonly been used for senior executives, sales staff and shopfloor employees involved in individual direct production. In these types of jobs there are measurable outputs (profits, sales, units of production) which are used to calculate the bonus payable. Normally payments are annual, quarterly, monthly or, in the case of shopfloor schemes, weekly. In the last few years, however, increasing numbers of employees have been put on to bonus schemes, partly as a substitute for, or as a complement to, merit pay.

Individual bonuses generally are categorised into two types:

a) *Incentives* – which pay out automatically for achievement of pre-set targets
b) *Rewards* – which pay out for performances which are subject to measurement or assessment after the event.

Incentives are normally seen as having the most direct impact on employee behaviour, while the impact of rewards is reduced by the degree of uncertainty which surrounds payment. Nonetheless, both types of bonus scheme have seen substantial growth in the last 10 years – about four out of five private sector executives now receive bonuses, compared with only one in five 10 years ago. Yet questioning the wisdom of individual bonuses is also common – do they have a positive impact on behaviour and are they a cost-effective reward?

To design effective schemes there are five key areas to consider:

a) the objectives
b) what bonuses are paid for
c) the amount
d) the distribution to employees
e) payment timing and frequency.

The Objectives

The objective of bonus schemes is often said to be 'improving individual performance by providing rewards for higher performance'. This is a statement of the obvious, but most schemes have more detailed aims when examined closely. For example, many support a focus on improving certain key aspects of performance (e.g. profit, return on capital employed, etc.) which are seen as important to shareholders. This means concentrating more effort on improving these aspects of performance rather than others, or counterbalancing some aspects of culture which strongly influence individual behaviour. For example, several of the recently privatised utilities have introduced bonus schemes linked to aspects of commercial and financial performance to support greater attention to cost-effective decision making and to encourage greater entrepreneurship. It is useful to think objectives through clearly because design for purpose is the key to the success of individual bonus schemes; vague objectives lead to muddled schemes.

What Bonuses Are Paid For

Individual incentive bonus schemes are paid against achieved measurable outputs; the important design issue is establishing appropriate outputs to reward. Although answers may sound obvious – sales for the sales person, earnings per share for the chairman, etc. – in practice all output measures need careful validation:

a) Is the measurable output really the best measure of performance for the individual in relation to the corporate performance
   requirement? There is a tendency in many schemes to assume
   that the individual has considerably more influence on the
   output than he or she actually has; no problem if the individual
   is prepared to accept the 'rough justice' implied, but a difficulty if the organisation wishes to communicate the bonus as
   being entirely under the individual's control. Similarly, many
   measures do not encapsulate what is really required in the
   job; in particular, quality or enduring customer relations may
   be as important as the quick sale. A good example of this is
   banking, where research shows[10] that profitability from customers increases with retention. Quick sales that subsequently
   lead to customer dissatisfaction need to be avoided, but direct
   sales incentives may encourage staff to 'make a sale' rather
   than 'build a relationship'.
b) Is the output measured robustly? The problem here is simply
   that many outputs can be achieved by doing the wrong thing
   for the organisation. For example, in the fast-moving consumer goods business a quick way to improve short-term
   profit is to reduce advertising spend, yet in the long run
   advertising spend is critical to growth.

Individual reward bonuses have similar design demands. Even
though they are post-hoc bonuses, they normally relate to pre-
set objectives against which it is possible to quantify success.
This requires sound objective setting and sound performance
evaluation.

In many respects, these requirements are similar to elements
of merit pay. It is not surprising, therefore, that several organisations (for example, Yorkshire Bank, Lloyds Bank and the Civil
Service) have individual bonus schemes that are directly linked
to their merit pay schemes so that performance rated at appraisal
may result in a base pay increase, a bonus or both.

The Bonus Amount

There are two conflicting considerations relating to individual
bonuses – to ensure that individual payments are large enough
to make a difference to people while at the same time limiting
the overall cost of the scheme to an acceptable level. As a rough

rule of thumb, most organisations believe that an individual bonus which pays out less than 5% of base salary is probably not worth it; the upper limit is really a matter of the degree of risk and the reward which is appropriate for the employee population. A bonus of 20% of base salary may seem a lot to a middle manager with no previous experience of variable pay, while in an entrepreneurial environment a bonus in excess of 50% may be the 'normal' level.

Organisations with individual bonus schemes take two approaches to amounts. *Unbudgeted approaches* define in advance how much individuals can receive for certain levels of performance, e.g.

Rating	Bonus
Objectives not met	No bonus
Met objectives	5% of salary
Exceeded some objectives	10% of salary
Exceeded all objectives	20% of salary

Budgeted approaches are where individuals share in a bonus pool generated by reference to company, division or unit performance; the share is then determined on a points basis linked to individual performance, e.g.

Pool		Individual Points	
Company Performance	Bonus Pool	Rating	Points
On budget	10% of salary bill	Exceptional	10
Below budget	0–10% of salary bill	Superior	7
Above budget	10–15% of salary bill	Satisfactory	5
		Incomplete	3
		Unsatisfactory	0

Say pool = £250,000
Total points = 1000
Each point = £250
Exceptional performer receives £2,500
Superior performer receives £1,750 etc.

The Distribution to Employees

An important design criterion is the number of employees who will be expected to receive a bonus. 'Elitist' schemes where only the very top people receive bonuses are less motivational to all employees than schemes where most employees can expect to earn a bonus. For the majority of 'average' performers 'elitist' schemes have no effect at all: earning a bonus is always out of reach. Nonetheless, many organisations with very little to spend on bonuses often concentrate resources on the very top performers. Yet unless the organisation is one where the stars really do drive performance a bonus scheme which motivates the average performer to do more is the most appropriate.

Payment Timing and Frequency

Individual bonus schemes have to link in with performance management cycles, not just performance appraisal but also the business planning cycle and the company's financial year. When these cycles are completed, bonuses should be made as quickly as possible to reinforce the link between performance and reward. This inevitably tends to make individual bonuses an annual event; but quarterly, or even monthly, payments are likely to be of greater value to many employees with short performance time horizons.

Group/Team Bonus

Group and team bonus schemes are designed to reward the performance of a specifically identified group or team of individuals in the organisation. The team has historically been the top or senior management group of the company, but with the advent of performance-related pay for wider tranches of employees this approach has become quite common in bonus schemes designed for employees in, for example, information technology, research and development, and customer service teams. In areas such as these individual performance pay in the form of bonuses is often strongly resisted. Not only can the identification and measurement of individual performance criteria be particularly difficult, but it is often divisive and counter to the team ethos which is such a vital and inherent component of most of the work undertaken.

Team schemes for the top or senior management group of the

company are introduced for subtly different reasons. For these jobs there is usually little difficulty in establishing key performance criteria for individual roles, many having clear responsibility for the financial results of an area of business operation within the company. The team ethos is not always seen as an integral part of these jobs. Indeed, it is precisely to reinforce and encourage the need for the top management to work as a team that such schemes are usually introduced. Many companies have found to their cost that incentive schemes which focus on individual performance criteria alone can encourage management to 'fight their own corner', to the detriment of the overall good of the organisation. Team bonus design is, in many respects, similar to individual bonus design. The additional requirements are:

a) *Ensuring that a team scheme is the most appropriate approach.* There are many circumstances where team bonuses are valid, but strong emphasis among employees on a team culture can mask problems of individual performance management. However, a well designed team scheme can also help address individual performance issues through the operation of supervisor or peer group pressure.

b) *Defining the eligible participants.* Although some groups are clearly identifiable, it can be difficult to come to an entirely satisfactory definition of a team. For example, in considering a team scheme for branch staff in a retail bank, it was not clearcut as to whether staff in supporting customer service centres should be excluded or included.

c) *Defining team performance.* Although many schemes use measures similar to those found in individual bonus schemes, team bonuses open up a wide range of possibilities. Project-based measures are not uncommon, and at lower levels in the organisation added value (gainsharing), productivity and output quality measures can be used.

d) *Determining payment levels for individuals.* A team scheme need not necessarily result in the same level of payments for all team members; some schemes may differentiate on the basis of job size, team responsibility level or individual performance.

Company-Wide Schemes

Schemes which link a part of total reward to the performance of the company are, technically speaking, a form of performance-related pay. However, they are not normally associated with individual performance management and are therefore dealt with fairly briefly here.

A company-wide performance-related pay scheme delivers separately identifiable rewards to all or some employees based on the achievement of one or more company performance targets, profit being the most common. Payments are typically annual or half-yearly, although some schemes pay out on a more frequent basis. Schemes may use cash or shares (or a combination and/or choice) as the currency for payment and as such encompass all forms of profit sharing.

Such schemes are not normally regarded as mechanisms for directly attempting to increase performance, although this may be an indirect result of such a scheme. The link between individual performance improvement and the operation of such schemes is tenuous. Remoteness from influence over the outcome and the infrequency of payments means that employees often regard them as a useful extra rather than an integral part of pay. Nonetheless, such schemes are felt to increase employee identity with the business as well as providing a useful communication vehicle regarding the importance of company performance for employees generally. The ability to link part of the payroll to company performance also provides useful cost flexibility in periods of performance downturn. Some company-wide schemes can also attract tax advantages for employees, notably profit-sharing schemes and profit-related pay.

Share Schemes

Like company-wide schemes, share option schemes, restricted stock schemes, employee share ownership plans (ESOPs) and employee share trusts represent an opportunity for performance reward to be linked to company fortunes. As a performance reward they have many of the disadvantages of company-wide schemes – remoteness from employee influence, lack of individual focus, etc. – but they are popular as a general reward and communication tool for all employees and are often viewed as a more instrumental incentive for executives. Indeed executive share option schemes have become the most popular form of long-term incentive for executives. However, their disadvantages are well known – executives feel they have little influence on the stock price and are likely to sell a large proportion of the shares soon afer options have been exercised. To overcome this disadvantage, restricted stock schemes linked to share ownership have begun to emerge in the UK, mirroring developments in the US. Share schemes, and long-term incentives generally, fall more within the province of executive remuneration policy; readers should turn to the relevant specialist literature.[11]

Incentive Gifts

Outside the sales and customer services areas, incentive gifts have hitherto been unpopular. However, holiday prizes, gifts from catalogues, 'Employee of the month' schemes and other non-cash rewards are now beginning to spread to other employee groups. For example, Albany Life, a small insurance company, has successfully introduced a catalogue gift scheme for back office support staff and the American practice of 'Employee of the month' has now spread into hotel, restaurant and retail chains in Britain.

These schemes have several advantages over cash; they are usually cheaper to operate than cash incentives and are specifically designed to have a motivational impact on non-winners as well as those in receipt of awards. Their drawback is their need to be constantly revitalised – each year something new may need to be added and eligibility rules changed. Before such schemes are written off as 'shopfloor'-based, it is interesting to note that some larger firms are now introducing special ties or badges for members of successful project teams in professional areas, as well as special pens and other 'high-class' office gifts associated with successful completion of key tasks.

Skills-Based Pay

Whether skills-based pay is a form of performance-related pay, or a grading system, depends on one's point of view. However, for certain groups of jobs, or job families, skills-based pay is increasing in popularity. It is a system which allows employees to progress through a range of grades based on their increasing skill, or competency, level. Performance management systems are built to evaluate and review skills levels achieved by employees and recommend grading changes. These systems normally apply over a range of grades below supervisory or management levels for clerical staff, systems analysts, computer programmers or sales and research teams.

Essential Ingredients for Making It Work

Although performance-related pay schemes may sound easy to implement and run, many schemes fail because the environment in which they are introduced is not favourable. Preliminary groundwork is essential for success; there are, particularly, five areas to cover prior to design:

1 *Understanding of what performance-related pay is and what it involves.* First and foremost, performance-related pay is not a neat, fail-safe mechanism divorced from the vagaries of human judgement that will automatically lead to improved performance and fairer rewards for all. It is a management tool, it gives management discretion and requires good sound judgement. It involves planning, managing, assessing and rewarding performance. It does not replace other aspects of people management; it reinforces it. It requires time, effort and resourcefulness. It will put pressure on the organisation's performance planning and budgeting processes, on management style and ability, and may highlight existing weaknesses. The prize for doing it well is getting more for the money spent in payroll. The idea that performance-related pay is a 'quick fix' has to be dispelled.

2 *Making sure it is introduced for the right reasons.* Performance-based reward is all about raising company performance through individual performance improvement. It cannot be a substitute for inadequate base pay. If an organisation feels that a group of individuals is underpaid for what they currently do, it would be better advised to increase base salaries than to introduce a performance-related pay scheme that is simply designed to increase total cash earnings. If employees see performance-related pay is only a facade they lose confidence in the process and it is extremely difficult to win them back.

3 *Gaining management commitment and trust in management.* As with most other aspects of pay, management must be committed to performance-related pay. Without this, any arrangements will not be implemented and maintained properly and will be unlikely to succeed. Similarly, performance-based rewards need to be introduced into an environment where employees have trust in their management. The message of performance-related pay cannot be communicated, and will not be listened to, unless employees can be convinced that it will be operated fairly and that managers will support employees in achieving higher levels of performance.

4 *Integrating the new scheme into the company's total reward strategy.* The total pay and benefits package must 'hang together' to provide a balanced system of rewards. Performance-related pay must fit in with this package. It is inadvisable, and usually wasteful, for performance-related pay to be tacked on to the existing pay package with insufficient attention given to resulting conflicts and inconsistencies. Different elements of the pay package address the issues of attraction, motivation and retention to varying degrees. It is critical to design a package that is balanced to achieve these aims. In choosing and determining the elements of performance-related pay, consideration needs to be given to the balance of variable and non-variable pay; rewards for individual, team and organisation contributions; discretionary rewards and rewards triggered automatically; cash rewards and non-cash rewards; and current and deferred pay.

5 *Tailoring it to the specific needs of the organisation.* Performance-related pay should be specific to an organisation: schemes can seldom be bought 'off the shelf'. It should reflect the business and how it is managed, its corporate culture and the people working within it. In light of these factors, choices need to be made about the types and levels of performance pay. To be cost-effective and motivational these schemes must be balanced and clearly linked to the way in which the performance of individuals is managed.

Characteristics of a Successful Scheme

Having established that performance-related pay is rightfully on the 'pay agenda', we turn to the five basic underpinnings of successful schemes:

Performance Criteria
Business objectives have to be translated into meaningful performance criteria for individuals or groups. Performance-related pay cannot work without good performance planning, management and assessment. Performance management arrangements that are only partially effective without the edge of pay are likely to crumble, or prove inadequate, if performance-related pay is added. But performance-related pay must run in tandem with performance management – to run a scheme separate from, or in conflict with, performance management doesn't work.

Job Definition
There must be a clear and shared understanding of the performance requirements of jobs by individuals and the company. Not
as they were or have been perceived to be, but as they are. In
addition, interdependencies with others in the organisation in
achieving objectives should be identified.

Payout Levels
Schemes must deliver significant rewards if they are to be taken
seriously and produce the desired motivational impact. Companies operating more than one scheme need to ensure that they
strike the right balance in terms of cash delivery. For example, if
there is a bonus scheme focused on achievement of two or three
specific objectives paying out 10 to 30% of base salary, and a
merit scheme based on whole job performance which delivers
maybe 4%, what is the overall message? A large number of
managers *say* that they are most concerned about encouraging
performance in a rounded sense but often do not put their money
there.

Differentiation
Schemes must offer sufficient differentials between levels of performance rating, otherwise high performers are inadequately
rewarded and average performers are insufficiently motivated
to improve. Many schemes fall down on this through lack of
confidence in management's ability to differentiate fairly. If individuals feel the scheme to be credible, fair and well managed
these differentials will not cause divisiveness and, indeed, will
be motivational.

Communication, Training and Review
Schemes must be properly communicated to individuals, with
the reasons for introduction clearly stated; appropriate training
is needed to ensure that the pay aspects are handled as well as
other aspects of performance management. A once-off exercise
is unlikely to be sufficient to ensure enduring success. The basic
messages of performance management and performance-related
pay need to be reinforced from time to time to help keep them
alive. Similarly, as with any element of pay, performance-related
pay arrangements need to be reviewed regularly to ensure that
they continue to be appropriate to the organisation's needs. Any
organisation that is not planning to look at annual out-turns, and
act on problems, will be storing up difficulties.

Steps in Introducing Performance-Related Pay

All too often organisations are tempted for one reason or another to rush the introduction of a performance pay scheme. The essential ingredients and characteristics for success discussed earlier are not just 'nice to have' comfort statements. They really do make the difference between performance-related pay becoming a valuable, accepted and integral part of the way in which the company manages and rewards people – and a waste of money.

It is easy to underestimate the resources (both time and money) that need to be utilised in arriving at the right solution for a particular company, and many senior managers do just that, anxious to see a scheme in place, for example, at the start of the next financial year. Drawn from the experiences of many organisations, the steps outlined below are intended to provide a framework of reference to any company considering the introduction of such a scheme:

1 *Establishing intent and objectives*
    a) Clearly define and gain top management agreement and commitment to *why* the company wants to introduce performance-related pay and what it hopes to achieve through it. This seems self-evident, but in practice it often does not happen; confusion and conflict can cloud the issue later on. The objective may be to improve the organisation's performance in some way; in which case, how? Or it may be viewed as a fairer way of allocating reward for the performance currently being delivered. Often it is a combination of the two.

    A clear statement of objectives has more benefit than simply providing a touchstone against which to determine whether and in what form performance-related pay will deliver the objectives. It helps to identify whether or not there are other forms of motivation and recognition the organisation could introduce as well as or instead, such as

    • improved career planning and development
    • improved training
    • non-cash forms of reward to recognise achievement.

    b) Determine the cost constraints. How much money will be available to fund the scheme and how much time, money and effort should be expended on designing, installing and implementing it? A common failure of performance-related pay schemes is that too much time is spent on the detailed design without having first established whether it fits appropriately with the organisation's culture and existing performance management processes. It is well worth spending a few tens of thousands of pounds to end up with the right scheme – which could cost hundreds of thousands or even millions of pounds once in operation.

c) Establishing whom the scheme will cover. At the outset, there are often fairly fixed views on whom the target population should be. It is important, however, to be prepared to be flexible on this. As developments unfold, it may prove that it is not sensible to include some jobs or that the lines for participation need to be redrawn.

2 *Planning design and implementation*

It is essential to determine who should be involved in design and implementation phases and arrive at an appropriate timetable. In their task of introducing performance-related pay, some organisations fail to involve sufficiently line managers, the finance department, the unions or the employees themselves. A realistic programme for involvement often results in a better scheme design.

3 *Managing expectations*

Managing expectations is an important step which is often overlooked altogether. It is unlikely that a successful performance-related pay scheme can be launched without individuals being aware for some time that the company is considering such an initiative. This is clearly true if their views are to be sought as part of the next diagnostic step.

In order not to raise expectations, it is advisable not to make an early announcement that a scheme will be introduced until the organisation has decided on at least the basic details. However, it normally is useful to communicate early on that the company is considering new or improved performance-related pay arrangements but that no firm decisions have as yet been taken.

4 *Diagnosis of readiness*

An assessment needs to be made of the existing systems and processes for managing pay and performance and the linkages between the two, and of other factors which need to be taken into consideration, such as culture and prevailing attitudes. A useful and quite powerful tool for achieving this is to conduct an employee attitude survey. This could take the form of a brief questionnaire, where participants are asked to identify the extent to which they agree or disagree with statements concerning the way in which their pay and performance is currently managed.

Some typical examples are:

- My manager is able to use the current pay system to motivate me
- Pay could be used more effectively to motivate me
- I am clear about the end results expected of me in my job
- I understand how my actions impact on the organisation's performance
- The appraisal process helps me to improve my performance
- The current appraisal system clearly differentiates on performance
- I expect an annual pay increase at least as much as inflation
- Employees who are better performers should receive meaningfully higher pay awards than average performers
- The current performance-related pay system encourages better individual performance
- It is clear how my annual performance appraisal links to my pay.

A diagnostic tool of this type is an effective way of gathering a comprehensive picture of the views and perceptions of a large number of individuals over a relatively short space of time. It can be of enormous benefit in helping to determine the likely impact of a performance-pay scheme and the current practices that need to be improved to ensure it works. Should such a survey be undertaken, however, the organisation must be prepared to feed back the results to the participants.

Whatever the methods used to assess the company's readiness for performance-related pay, it is vital to be prepared to accept that now may not be the right time to go ahead. It may, for example, be prudent to spend the forthcoming year on improving the company's ability to define, manage and assess the performance of individuals or groups and introduce the performance-related pay element at a later stage.

5 *Detailed design*

As was shown earlier, there is a wide choice of performance-related pay arrangements available. It is necessary to go through a rigorous refinement of options, looking at the fit that schemes have with organisational needs. Having done this, detailed design work on eligibility, measurement, links with other aspects of performance management, pay-out arrangements and communication needs to be undertaken. As part of the design it is desirable to model 'what ifs' to check the financial robustness of the scheme and generate figures for employees, setting out the risk level associated with variable payments.

6 *Implementation*

   a) *Training* Depending on the type of scheme or schemes being introduced and the state of readiness of the organisation, a training programme is likely to be needed to develop line management's ability both to set appropriate and meaningful performance targets and to manage individuals' performance during the year towards achieving them. Even if managers are accustomed to conducting performance appraisal, further training may be necessary as the introduction of performance-related pay will put an edge on the appraisal process.

   b) *Communications* A communications strategy should be developed alongside the design of the scheme. It is critical that all concerned understand how the scheme will operate and why it is being introduced. The programme may include a booklet as well as presentations to groups of employees by line management, personnel managers or consultants.

   c) *Quality checks* A process for ensuring that the scheme is being equitably applied throughout the organisation is critical if it is to be robust and seen as fair and motivating to all employees.

   d) *Monitoring and Review* As with any other human resource initiatives, performance-related pay arrangements need to be regularly reviewed to ensure they are operating as intended and continue to meet the needs and objectives of the business. Particularly in the initial stages some unforeseen difficulties are likely to occur no matter how thoroughly the scheme has been thought through. Be prepared to make modifications and improvements in the scheme in the light of these.

Conclusions

So is performance-related pay worth it? The weight of opinion is clearly moving towards performance becoming a more identifiable, and larger, part of pay arrangements. In the 1980s many organisations progressed up the difficult learning curve of managing such pay arrangements. The main messages from them are:

a) Don't look at performance-related pay as a 'quick fix'; integrate it with other performance management initiatives
b) Be clear about objectives, and work to achieve them through sound design, implementation and review
c) Look at performance-related pay as part of wider initiatives on performance management and within the context of overall reward strategies
d) Constantly work at improving performance-related pay; left to decay, schemes will eventually lose their direction and impact.

The expectation, given the structure of business in Britain, is that performance-related pay will spread still further in the 1990s. The success of such changes in improving the performance of 'Britain Limited' remains to be tested.

6

Counselling and Coaching

by Tricia Allison

Give a man a fish and he will be fed for a day,
Teach a man to fish and he will be fed forever
–author unknown

The terms 'coaching' and 'counselling' are constantly bandied about in organisations when problems and stresses occur. Sometimes they are used almost interchangeably. 'Counselling' often refers to processes such as coaching which bear no relation to the work of professional counsellors. Yet the basic distinction is clear. In the situation described in the above proverb, showing a man where to get a fish would be an example of *coaching*; helping him to survive by building on the experience of knowing how to fish and growing from it would count as *counselling*.

The prime aim of this chapter is to focus on the process of counselling in performance management, the difference between short course basic counselling skills and the skills which professional counsellors have to offer to both individuals and organisations. The benefit for managers of being able to use basic counselling skills in order to assist employees to maintain and regain satisfactory levels of performance is illustrated both by the inclusion of pointers to watch out for and by a case study drawn from actual experience.

The secondary aim of this chapter is to re-establish the distinction between the processes of counselling and coaching, by examining first the current problems and stresses to be found for managers and individuals in organisations, and the managerial role in reducing those stresses. The differences between counselling and coaching will then be defined before looking at coaching in more detail.

Having established the benefits of employee counselling, the Post Office's initiative in this area is illustrated in a case study. The chapter concludes by considering what managers need to address when wishing to introduce such a service into an organisation.

Organisational and Individual Stress

As organisations become more competitive, additional pressures are heaped on all employees at all levels. Managers are under pressure not only to achieve results but also to become more sophisticated in the way they handle their staff. As the incidence of stress-related conditions escalates, a manager has to know how to respond to problems such as anxiety, depression and alcohol abuse, which may all contribute towards poor performance.

Company directors frequently assert that their most important resource is 'people'. Yet how often do organisations protect, support or nurture this most valuable asset? The effectiveness of any organisation depends upon the individuals who form it. People respond to being valued, to being made to feel important, as well as to being rewarded when a job is done well. The Industrial Society report *Blueprint for Success* (1989)[1] revealed that pay rated only fourth in the top five most important aspects of a job. At the head of the list by far was job satisfaction and inherent in this was good communication.

The structure and ethos of an organisation affects individual behaviour. A style can be set and emanates from the top. If that style reflects a humanitarian attitude, if there is a respect for health and wellbeing as well as for productivity and performance, it is more likely that there will be a committed workforce. Employees are quick to feel that 'If the company doesn't care about us, why should we care about it?' In the current demographic climate, the level of employee commitment may be crucial to organisational survival.

Managers who normally cope well with their own stress at work may themselves unwittingly be the instigators of stress in others, by imposing unreasonable deadlines or requiring staff to undertake tasks for which they have either not been adequately trained or they lack the necessary expertise. In such circumstances a member of staff may experience the same feelings of impotence and inability to cope as some managers experience when the 'plane is grounded at Heathrow due to fog and the chance of attending an important meeting becomes nil. In both instances stress is associated with feelings of being unable to control, contain or remedy the situation.

What then can be done to reduce the impact of stress? First of all, there are certain basic principles which the organisation must accept. These are that:

- Some employee problems are caused by the company itself
- Managers need to be taught a range of skills to cope with such problems
- If these problems are ignored, the company will bear the cost in terms of absence, inefficiency, poor performance, high accident levels, early retirement and increased recruitment and training.[2]

A company which had the courage to assess the way it created or compounded personnel problems was Thorn EMI, Technology Group, which was concerned about the high drop-out rate among new recruits – 40% were being lost within their first year of employment. An exit study of new entrants revealed that the major reason for departure was the feeling of too much pressure. This emanated from factors such as poor supervision, hierarchical corporate structures and management styles which discouraged free discussion and penalised failure. Thorn faced the problem by instituting workshops for managers on how to channel pressure positively.[3]

Similarly, ITT World Directories (UK) Ltd dealt with their problem of staff retention in their sales area by introducing an employee assistance service (initially on a trial basis) in their Manchester Region. A 100% turnover in the sales force in 1985 had reduced to 40% in 1990, coupled with a dramatic improvement in attendance levels.[4]

The Managerial Role

The relationship between employee and boss is generally recognised to be the most important in the work environment and yet for many managers (many of whom attained their status as a result of pure technical ability), managing people is a major source of stress. Couple with this the fact that the average manager's longest interaction with any one individual in a day is six minutes and there is no doubt that opportunities are constantly being lost.[5]

Employee development may be seen as a corporate responsibility which in the day-to-day context is delegated to the manager. However, it is important to recognise that this responsibility must also be shared by the employee: learning cannot take place without the commitment of the individual concerned. The nature of the learning may be about the job or about self. The managerial role in the first instance is likely to be that of coach, in the second that of counsellor.

Counselling or Coaching

Three years ago a group of 10 senior managers who had recently retired from their organisation underwent a basic counselling skills training course. The purpose was to equip them to act as helpers to current employees who were to be displaced as a result of business restructuring. They found the experience both stimulating and rewarding, but their positive feelings were tinged with enormous regret. They even felt cheated. 'If only we had had a course like this years ago when we started as managers, how much difference it would have made. All this time, what we thought was counselling wasn't counselling at all!' So what *are* the differences between counselling and coaching?

Counselling is about helping people to manage their lives effectively. It is a process of helping them find and achieve what *they* want in life. Their desired outcomes may not be yours. As a manager this can sometimes be difficult to accept. In coaching, the manager is heavily involved in the definition of objectives and needs, in counselling it is for the individual to determine these. Coaching is work-related and problem-centred, while counselling is more about the person and the person's feelings. Coaching is often a more public affair than counselling, which has strong boundaries of confidentiality. The coaching role has no limitations for the line manager, the counselling role does (is it appropriate to know the detail of an employee's private life and, in any case, would they tell you?). The coaching relationship contains differentials of power whereas counselling is about meeting as equals, two human beings, one of whom is acting as an enabler by using communication skills which allow the other to feel safe, understood and accepted.

Coaching

Although formal training is appropriate for the acquisition of specific theoretical, technical or conceptual knowledge, individuals learn most from day-to-day application of skills, by trying things out in practice. If these learning experiences arc controlled and feedback is provided by managers who understand the job and can identify needs, then quality and speed of learning are enhanced. The results are greater job satisfaction, greater enthusiasm and improved performance on the part of the employee.

This, in essence, is coaching using everyday work, together with discussion and planned activity, as a learning experience for people. But coaching, like counselling, with which it is often confused, is a skill which has to be learned. It is thus incumbent upon the organisation to ensure that managers are given appropriate training to acquire these skills.

The basic components of coaching have been described as:

- dealing essentially with the development of skill through practice
- analysing the components of particular skills, techniques and the environment in order to assist the learners
- setting increasingly challenging exercises
- seeking to identify problems or weaknesses to be remedied
- spotting potential, building on strengths and taking advantage of talent and opportunity.[6]

It thus aims at improving both current and future performance. It requires joint commitment to mutually accepted goals coupled with a plan of action for achieving them.

Good coaching requires a supportive, consultative approach and well developed listening skills: it is important to hear accurately not only what has been said, but also what has not been said. The practice of summarising and reflecting back what was said, at appropriate intervals, is a valuable means of checking this accuracy. The listening process is assisted by creating an environment which encourages the learner to open up: by talking where one will not be interrupted, by using good eye contact, by using prompting words and nods and by adopting a posture which conveys full attention. How many of us have in our time felt totally unheard by the person whose actions and body language convey both lack of regard and interest? The person who, for example, looks everywhere but at you, who continues to read items from the in-tray and takes repeated telephone calls in what is intended to be *your* time? Does this encourage positive sharing?

Key to the coaching process is the effective use of a range of question styles. For example, *probing questions* aid the understanding of the learner's thinking and reasoning; *checking questions* allow the person to expand on a topic; *challenging questions* encourage a second look at ideas and methods, perhaps allowing for change; *prompting questions* allow the learner to explore a number of options before deciding upon a particular course of action; and *open questions* (what, when, where, how and why?) place the onus on the learner to think issues through, rather than simply being able to answer 'yes' or 'no'. While fact-finding is an important component in coaching, the ability to draw out broader ideas and thoughts helps the learner to review implications and examine possibilities.

Coaching is a long-term strategy. In the short term, when a manager is under time pressure, it may feel more expedient either to undertake a task oneself or to simply issue a precise set of instructions. However, while this approach may achieve the immediate objective, it fails to develop individual performance. It neither stretches people nor expands their roles.

The opportunities for coaching are numerous. They may arise as the result of promotion, job restructuring, job rotation, holiday relief, system changes, secondment and, not least, planned delegation of part of the manager's own job. Creating a special project assignment also opens up avenues.

The first step in the process is to identify need. What evidence is there of current job performance as a result of the performance appraisal procedure? What aspects cause difficulty? What objectives are not met? What changes or challenges are likely to occur during the next six or 12 months? What are the individual's perceptions? Can he/she also identify what changes need to take place, what the areas are for improvement?

Thus targets can be agreed, ground rules and time scales set. How often will progress be reviewed and how long will reviews take? Who else will be affected and who else can help? Once these decisions have been reached, there is a responsibility on the part of the manager to ensure that all necessary information is available to the learner and that potential problems have been considered. It is important to build and support the person's confidence while also stimulating independent thinking and action. Intervention should be necessary only if a critical situation develops.

Learning can be completed only with effective, objective feedback from the coach. At points of review it can be helpful to ask the learner's opinion of what has been learned and how specific aspects could have been handled differently. Very often people know these things without being told: it is not uncommon for the learner to be more critical of self than the coach will be. Concentration should be on action and behaviour and, whether feedback involves commendation or criticism, it must always be positive, constructive and sensitive. Negative feedback simply raises the defences and the learner ceases to hear.

It should not be forgotten that the benefits of coaching are two-way. Helping others to learn is one of the best ways of developing one's own learning. The skills used in effective coaching are communication, motivation, delegation, planning and monitoring. They are precisely those required to be a successful manager. 'Every success I've ever had came about because I was trying to help other people. . . Every promotion I got came about when I was up to my ears helping my associates to be effective as possible. . .' (Robert Townsend, *Up the Organisation*).

Counselling

The task of counselling is to assist others to make changes in their work or life, or to accept or adjust to the change which they are experiencing in a way that, without counselling, they are finding difficult or impossible. The purpose is not to advise, but to provide the vehicle for individuals to achieve their own solutions to their problems.

The process is one of helping people to voice concerns; come to terms with their own feelings; understand their own motives, values and aspirations more clearly; and assess options and make choices between them. It is about helping them to draw on their own strengths and mobilise their own energies, in order to make changes and take effective action. The process also helps people to feel more in control of their lives, and able to do something about situations, feelings or relationships, rather than simply experiencing helplessness. Furthermore, by working through either the making of an important choice or a distressing crisis, counselling can help people to develop their ability to deal with future difficulties. It is useful not simply in alleviating a crisis, but also in allowing people to think their way more clearly through change points such as career development or retirement.

Counselling, like coaching, is not a new phenomenon. Good managers have always been alive to the impact of personal problems and emotional conflicts on job performance and satisfaction, and have sought to offer an appropriate ear. The line manager is often best placed to recognise the individual with a problem, and it may be that intervention at an early stage can prevent things escalating to the point where the problem becomes chronic and where performance is either seriously impaired or absence occurs. However, it is possible that the problem may be more complex than the manager feels able or competent to handle, in which case basic counselling skills can be used to encourage the employee to seek further help from someone more appropriate: perhaps a professional counsellor or other specialist.

The extensive use of counselling skills, and the provision of formal counselling facilities for employees, can have great impact on the reduction of stress, thereby helping employees to remain effective and productive. It represents a 'caring face' in a climate where employees all too easily see themselves as devalued to the level of cogs in a wheel. It also represents an organisational investment in health and wellbeing. The dividends in return are commitment, motivation, good performance, loyalty and staff retention.

Sometimes a manager may feel reluctant to engage in a counselling role, even if a problem is perceived. There may simply be an unwillingness to become involved, but it could also be the result of feelings of inadequacy to deal with whatever issues may arise: there is an oft-expressed fear of opening 'Pandora's box' and then not knowing what to do. There may also be a fear about how to handle the emotions which may be revealed. Sometimes lack of time is seen as a factor. There will inevitably be occasions too, when an individual's managerial role will be in conflict with that of counselling:

> As a manager it's my responsibility to get the show on the road . . . to sell advertising space . . . and make a profit. But as a manager I realise that I also have a responsibility towards the people who work in the department. I do want them to feel that they can come to me with any problem, whether it be something at work related to their actual job, their surroundings, or even a personal problem. But there does come a time when I don't want to get too involved in their personal situation. If I get too involved it makes my job very difficult. . . I can get involved to a degree . . . but if I find that I am getting out of my depth, I would refer them on to the counsellor. (Lesley Webb, Classified Advertisement Manager, *The Sunday Times*.)[7]

Managers have certain work objectives to achieve. Their primary interest is in the effective running of their operation and the welfare of the company. It may be that the achievement of business objectives may not be in the best interests of the individual, and sometimes this causes conflict. Equally, there is the important issue of confidentiality, which imposes limitations for manager and employee alike. Managers cannot guarantee confidentiality, and staff may have severe difficulties in accepting the manager as someone to whom they can freely reveal themselves, for fear of information being used against them. This also applies to their approaching a personnel manager. However, the confidentiality problem can be solved by agreeing boundaries at the very outset. It is then clearly understood by both parties which areas may remain confidential, and what information would have to be passed on and to whom.

To recognise the limitations of counselling in the workplace is vital, because it sets parameters and allows managers to practise counselling skills within a framework of reality. It is extremely stressful to feel under an obligation to handle all situations. Just as the counselling ethos creates a climate in which it is regarded as normal to have problems, it must also convey the message that it is acceptable for a manager to feel unable to assist in certain instances. The important aspect then becomes appropriate assistance in gaining help elsewhere.

Who can benefit from counselling? It is widely accepted that 20% of any workforce at any given time is troubled, so the realistic answer is that, at some time or another, most of us would gain from the opportunity. However, when making an assessment as to who might be in need of counselling, there are certain indicators which may assist in deciding to offer it.

One of the soundest clues to an individual being under severe stress is change in behaviour. People are fairly predictable in their day-to-day behaviour, and both managers and colleagues get to know how they will behave in certain circumstances. Any disruption to this general pattern may be significant. Equally, changes in health, habits and work performance may be a key. Some examples of changes which may occur are:

- increased irritability
- loss of concentration
- decrease in output
- withdrawal from social interaction
- poor timekeeping
- increased absence
- failure to meet performance targets
- failure to meet deadlines
- inability to make decisions
- inability to respond to motivation
- inability to handle situations which normally present no difficulty
- lack of energy and enthusiasm
- displays of anxiety and tension.

Picking up on such signs, and taking 20 or 30 minutes to acknowledge with the person that they are going through a difficult time, will in itself help them to feel understood and perhaps precipitate the process of recovery.

The Skills of Counselling

There are many different styles of counselling, but research suggests that style is not of great importance, so long as the relationship between the counsellor and the individual being counselled is one which is appropriate for producing change. However, the style most generally used to train people in counselling skills is that of client-centred counselling, based on the work of Carl Rogers (1951)[8] and techniques developed from it by Gerard Egan (1986).[9] These techniques are fairly readily learned and thus provide a good foundation. The style is also relatively safe: a common fear among people when they begin to use counselling skills is that they will in some way damage the individual.

Perhaps one of the most helpful books on the subject is *The Manager's Guide to Counselling at Work* (1987),[10] which clearly explains and demonstrates the skills involved in Egan's three-stage counselling model. At this point, though, it is appropriate to strike a cautionary note. When Egan ran a workshop in London in July 1990 for the Independent Counselling and Advisory Service (ICAS), he stressed a fear that the very success of his own book, *The Skilled Helper*, was destroying the counselling profession. He voiced his concern that people fail to move beyond stage-one skills: 'They latch on to communication and counselling skills and think that they are counsellors.' The content of most short training courses is very much concentrated on those stage-one skills of active listening, facilitative questioning, reflection, summarising and feedback.

The counselling relationship is the main vehicle for growth and change, but there are three basic conditions which need to be established before development can occur:

- The first is acceptance: complete acceptance of individuals as they are, in a non-judgemental way which makes them feel valued. This acceptance (known in Rogerian terms as unconditional positive regard) is not always easy to achieve. The first step in trying to do so is to attempt to see the world through the eyes of the individual: it enables a better understanding of that person's motivations and thus behaviour.
- Second, the counsellor must genuinely be him- or herself.

Everything about the counsellor must ring true, there must be no hiding behind a role. Straightforwardness and sensitivity are crucial.

- The third condition is empathy: the active process of under-standing and feeling *with* rather feeling *sympathy for* the person. Being empathetic means engaging in a sharing with the person, thus creating a trusting environment in which they feel secure enough to talk about things which they dare not talk about to anybody else, sometimes even themselves.

An effective counsellor listens more than he talks and what he does say confirms for the client that he is being heard and under-stood. The counsellor's role involves helping the client to explore his world and so to sort out his own confusion. It is not the counsellor's role to choose the direction in which the client moves, but rather to provide the environment in which the client can best decide where to go. The counsellor then accompanies him on his journey of exploration. As a counsellor, allow your client to go where his current energy is taking him rather than trying to lead him in a particular direction. When the client has learnt to trust you, and to know that you will listen to the trivial, then he will feel safe enough to venture towards the real source of his pain. In other words, if you stay with the trivial, the important will emerge.[11]

'Barry' – A Case Study

Barry is an executive officer in the operational division of his organisation. He is in his mid–20s and has always been assessed as an able employee with a good deal of potential. However, people are beginning to doubt this assessment. He has consist-ently failed to meet required performance standards and his department heads feel that they can no longer afford to 'carry' him. People have commented that he seems to spend a lot of his lunch hours in the pub. Three months ago he incurred a four-week period of sick absence for which the medical certificates read 'depression'. He is interviewed by his boss, who informs him he is still not pulling his weight, and that he must get his act together quickly or else he will have to be moved off the job. Period.

Fortunately for Barry, he is seen by a perceptive member of the organisation's occupational health service, who is able to use basic counselling skills to discover enough to feel that he is in need of more specialist help. He is not altogether sure about this, and wonders what good it will really do, but he's worried about the job situation and somewhat reluctantly agrees to a referral to the professional counsellor. He doesn't suppose there is anything to lose.

The first session with the counsellor is quite a long one (it is usual for them to last about an hour). He is amazed at how much there is to talk about once he starts. He admits to opening up about things he has never discussed before. Some of them feel quite alarming to him, but are less so once they have been voiced. When he was off with depression his doctor put him on medication, but this had finished. He has not seen the doctor since, although he is feeling far from himself. In piecing it all together with the counsellor it becomes clear to them both that the depression is by no means behind him.

Barry sees his depression as being entirely work-related. He has had to carry two jobs for an extended period and, in addition, the most senior manager in the unit gives little support, appearing to be counting the days to retirement. At the time immediately prior to his sickness absence, he was also coping with the day-to-day duties of a further manager, as well as contending with major organisational changes which directly impacted on his department.

This stress has had terrible ramifications upon his personal life. He has not been able to sleep properly for ages and tries to induce it by drinking heavily every evening. He cannot talk to his wife and feels that he is driving her away. Their sexual relationship is non-existent. He wouldn't blame her if she left him. After all, is he worth staying with? He is perpetually irritable and has lost his sense of humour. All in all, life is an incredible mess. He used to enjoy it, but not any more. In addition his Dad died a few months ago – no warning, a heart attack. He also moved house, his wife changed job, there are increased financial pressures and their last holiday had to be cancelled because there was too much work to do on the new house. At times he has contemplated suicide.

It is a revelation to Barry that all these events are regarded by the counsellor as significant. He begins to feel reassured by the knowledge that there are in fact good reasons for his stress symptoms and resultant malfunctioning. He has considered only aspects of his life (i.e. work) which were immediately impacting on him at the time his sickness absence began. He hadn't realised that stress is often caused by a build-up of pressure over a period of many months, sometimes years.

Barry and the counsellor arrange to meet again in a week's

time. In the meantime she gives him a stress rating scale to take away and complete. She feels that it may be helpful for him to gain an objective measure as to the degree of stress he could be expected to experience.

The following week, Barry is already significantly improved. His mood is more optimistic and he feels that he is beginning to 'get a grip on things again'. He has been able to talk to his wife about last week's session. He feels that perhaps there is light at the end of the tunnel. He chooses to use this session to talk about how he may be able to handle the work situation better.

By the third session, a fortnight later, Barry feels that he has made huge progress. He says that understanding the causes of his depression has been the key. He is performing well at work and has been told so. He coped well when his boss was on leave last week and he feels enthusiastic again. He is no longer drinking excessively and he feels happy once more. There has been positive comment from his managers and his wife about the improvement, and he and the counsellor reach the conclusion that there is no further need for them to meet unless he wishes to do so at any time in the future.

This account is entirely accurate. The only aspect which has been changed is the client's name. The case was chosen because it is an example of a very common kind of situation which presents itself as a counselling problem at work. With appropriate help, stress is eminently treatable.

The Post Office – A Case Study

The idea of a specialist counselling facility within the Post Office was formulated by the then Chief Medical Officer, Dr Michael McDonald. In 1984, he advised the setting up of a working party to identify the needs of Post Office staff in respect of specialist counselling for stress, and a report was duly presented the following year. The working group included a range of opinion and experience in both the counselling and health education fields, as well as in the operation and resourcing of the work of the Post Office as a whole.

It was acknowledged that the Post Office already offered first-line counselling support to employees through the nursing and welfare services. The *specialist* role was to deal with more complex and deep-seated psychological problems of the kind which perhaps would previously have been referred outside the Post

Office. These were to include the areas of alcohol, drugs and stress.

Consequently, for the three years 1986–89, The Post Office, in a pilot study on stress counselling, made the first major attempt by any company in the UK to evaluate the effects of offering employees professional counselling for stress-related problems. The study took place in the organisation's North East and North West regions, and was conducted under the supervision of Professor Cary Cooper of the University of Manchester Institute of Science and Technology (UMIST).

The project was timed to coincide with a major reorganisation within the business and was also a direct response to the problem of stress-related absences in the Post Office, first identified some 10 years earlier. For the duration of the project, there were two counselling posts, based in Leeds and Manchester, each with catchment populations of 6/7000 staff. They were located within the Occupational Health Service.

Referrals

Over the three years there were approximately 600 referrals. The detailed UMIST analysis concentrates on a sample of the first 249. It was an open access service, and the client base ranged from cleaners through to senior managers. The male:female ratio was 70:30. The bulk of referrals were from occupational health (40%), followed by self-referral (31%) and welfare (19%). The remaining 10% came from such areas as management, personnel and trade unions. Few referrals were inappropriate and many were extremely complex.

The major cluster of work was in the broad category of stress and mental health, accounting for 49% of the caseload. These clients normally presented with anxiety and/or depression. Of the remaining 51% of referrals, the second most significant group was that surrounding relationship problems (25%), with the majority focusing on marital difficulties. Other areas included alcoholism and addictions, bereavement and assault. Work issues formed 10%.

An analysis of perceived sources of pressure at work showed organisational structure or climate to be the greatest problem, followed by factors intrinsic to the job and relationships with other people. As a means of assessing the severity of cases, account was taken of the proportion of individuals who had considered suicide. Risk was present, in varying degrees, in 25%

of cases. The grouping included people who had already made an attempt to terminate their lives.

The counselling service could be described as efficient. The counsellors provided a rapid and brief intervention for a large proportion of clients, resulting in broadly satisfactory outcomes. Some 50% were seen within five days of referral, 90% within 10 days. Some 70% of the sample were handled within four sessions, and of that percentage 34% required only one session. Within the work setting, employees have a high motivation to resolve their problems, so counselling sessions tended to be productive.

Evaluation of the Project

Evaluation focused on two areas:

– effectiveness from an organisational viewpont
– effectiveness from an individual angle.

At the organisational level, objective measures of sickness absence data were collected for the six months prior to counselling and for the six months following closure of the case. At the individual level, various psychological variables were examined using questionnaires derived from the Crown Crisp Experiential Index (1979)[12] and Warr, Cook and Wall (1979).[13] These were given to employees at the time of the first interview with the counsellor and then repeated once the case had been closed.

The measurements covered levels of:

– anxiety
– somatic anxiety (e.g. loss of appetite, sleeplessness, constant tiredness)
– depression
– self-esteem
– job satisfaction
– organisational commitment
– methods of relaxation (e.g. smoking, drinking, talking to someone).

An analysis of scores obtained from the client group, compared with a control group of employees, showed that employees seeking counselling were more anxious, depressed, suffered more physical complaints, had lower self-esteem, lower job satisfaction and lower organisational commitment than the random group of

Post Office employees. The client group, therefore (as one might expect), suffered poor psychological health when they entered counselling. After counselling they showed improvements in all areas of psychological wellbeing and also significant changes in behaviour (see Figure 6.1). They also drank less coffee, smoked less and used alcohol less as a coping mechanism. They exercised more and used relaxation techniques with effect. After counselling, the client group's scores more closely approximated to the control group's.

In terms of sickness absence, there was a substantial average reduction of 66% after counselling. This compares with an increase of 10% within the control group (see Figure 6.2). Using 177 clients, it was possible to estimate a saving of £101,993 on the basis of average daily salary for respective grades. A full cost-benefit analysis was not undertaken but may be assumed to be considerably higher.

What to Consider on Introducing an Employee Counselling Service

> I think within 10 years it will be commonplace to be running Employee Assistance Programmes (EAPs). The labour market is going to get tighter and tighter, employees will look for this [an EAP] when they look at the benefits a company has to offer. They'll look to see if there's a company car, if there's BUPA, and other benefits, to see if it's a caring company. They will see that it is if there is an Employee Assistance Programme in place. (Ian Anderson, Community Affairs Manager, Whitbread.)[7]

Employee counselling services may be in-house or external. They may focus on specific problems (e.g. alcohol and other substance abuse), or they may be 'broad brush'. They may be direct-access (where employees can refer themselves), or indirect-access (where employees have to be referred by someone such as a line or personnel manager).

Whatever type of service an organisation chooses, there are two essential prerequisites for its successful introduction: that there should be support from senior management, unions and staff associations, for the concept of counselling in the workplace, and that the service should be available to employees at all levels. Companies need to recognise that, rather than being a drain on the economic resources of an organisation, the introduction of appropriate counselling services can no longer be ignored. As

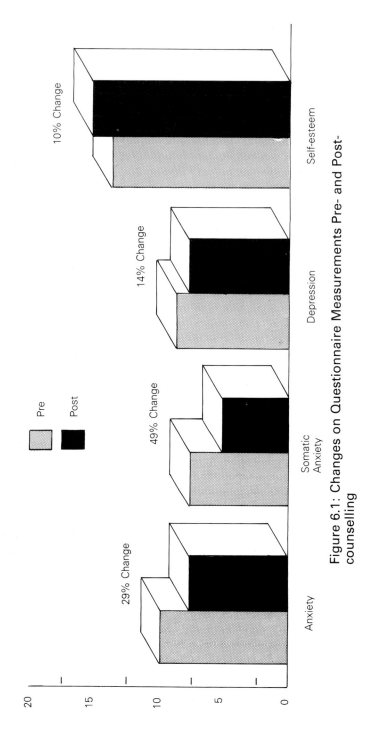

Figure 6.1: Changes on Questionnaire Measurements Pre- and Post-counselling

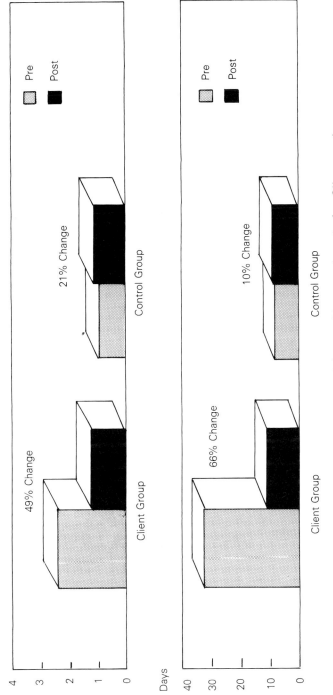

Figure 6.2: Pre- and Post-sickness Absence Levels for Client and Control Groups

companies will increasingly compete for a limited human resource, they need not only to attract potential employees, but also to retain them and maintain performance levels. According to Peter Saville, an occupational psychologist and Director of Saville and Holdworth Ltd, 33% of work performance is impaired by personal problems.[14]

Counselling at work represents good personnel practice and pays off in bottom-line cost savings. In the USA eight out of 10 top companies employ counsellors and it is estimated that for every dollar invested in counselling, *at least three* are saved. Further statistics reveal that:

- of those employees who are suffering impaired performance, 6% will be seriously disabled by their problem(s)
- 40% of absenteeism is due to mental/emotional problems (HMSO, 1988)
- approximately 30 million working days per annum are lost due to psychoneurotic disorders, and another 10 million due to other stress related illnesses, all at a cost of approximately £3,000 million
- approximately £700 million is lost each year through alcohol-related absences, and death through alcoholism cost UK industry £1.3 billion in 1986. 5% of male and 2% of female employees may have an alcohol problem
- Coronary Heart Disease (CHD) is responsible for a third of male and a quarter of female deaths in the UK each year: one person every three to four minutes. CHD costs an organisation of 10,000 employees almost £2 million per annum in lost productive value (British Heart Foundation)
- presenteeism (where someone's body is at work, but the mind is elsewhere) is probably more expensive than absenteeism.[15]

As the Health and Safety Executive report, *Mental Health at Work* (HMSO, 1988), reflects, 'Even a small reduction of this [catalogue of disasters] would be of considerable financial benefit to an employer.'[16]

In considering the appropriateness of an employee counselling service for any organisation, the first step is to identify need. Is there a need? Are you certain? Can you prove it? Can you persuade others? Is the company big enough to sustain a provision? (In America in January 1991 48% of all companies had an EAP.)[17] In order to answer these questions it can be helpful, possibly with the assistance of a consultant, to conduct an attitude survey, to examine occupational health records, turnover and absence levels.

Having established the need, one should consider the merits of both internal and external providers. There should be no fundamental difference between them. In order to maintain confidentiality both must be independent of the line management structure. Some people might feel that this is easier to achieve if the service is external.

The ICAS report, *Counselling Services in UK Organisations* (1989)[18] reveals that nearly twice as many employees were visiting counsellors who were visibly separate from the decision-making process of the company than those who had other company responsibilities such as personnel management. However, if counsellors are internal to an organisation, they should be employed at a sufficiently senior grade to carry 'clout'. As I found from personal experience as an internal counsellor for both the Trustee Savings Bank and the Post Office, being recognised as an influential voice is most important.

A benefit to an internal resource is greater ownership of the function: access to information and people, and a thorough understanding of the company's working methods and culture. The relationship between any company and counselling service provider has to be open and trusting and the referrals voluntary. Progress may seem relatively slow. Stress has until recently been seen as symptomatic of weakness, madness or incapacity, and companies cannot change their culture overnight.

An advantage of using an external provider is that there is no relationship to protect, no need to become personally involved. It may be easier for the external resource to stand its ground, not to bend to company pressure. Certainly, where a company management style has a strong need to control, and where 'control' means 'knowing', then it may be easier for everyone if the service is external: managers accept what they cannot control more readily when it does not come under their direct jurisdiction.

Formal counselling is, as has been indicated, a highly skilled task, and professional standards are crucially important: *no* counselling service may be preferable to a bad one. Professional qualifications and experience are vital for anyone employed as a full-time counsellor, as this will provide the assurance of a code of practice. The issue of confidentiality precludes a great deal of sharing, and so often the role and process of counselling is little understood by others. No professional counsellor, however experienced, should be prepared to operate without regular casework consultation. Also, company counsellors will require the capacity to 'market' the service, to develop policies and training programmes, and to understand the realities of organisational and industrial life. They have to be aware of how managerial decisions may impact on a client and the counselling process.

Gaining and maintaining confidentiality is the basis of any counselling service or, as previously stated, the service will not be used. The essential feedback to the organisation regarding trends, problem areas and the extent to which the service is being used can be presented in statistical form.

Fundamental to the service is the establishment of the principle that employees may receive counselling help within working hours. In the case of an internal service the location of a counsellor's office is thus of prime importance. Access must be as private as possible. If people choose to be open about using the service, that is their decision; it should not be thrust upon them.

There must be provision of appropriate support staff. Paperwork cannot be processed through a typing pool and selection of secretarial and clerical support must be undertaken with extreme care.

In choosing an external counselling resource, it is important to consider the 'track record' of the provider. What is its reputation, its history, its reliability, its specific industry knowledge? How does it measure its performance and what are the feedback mechanisms? What are its range of services (does it deal with global problems from plumbing to legal issues or specifically professional counselling)? If a global service, what is the quality of onward referral for counselling? Is it user-friendly? How is contact made by the employee? Does it offer 24-hour, 365-day coverage or are there restrictions?

Finally, when the nature of the counselling service is determined, the quality of its launch is important. Successful introduction of such a venture will involve education and training within the company, and adequate publicity in the shape of brochures, posters and newsletters. It is important to ensure that appropriate awareness levels are reached for the service to succeed.

With the growing acknowledgement within organisations of the benefits of demonstrating their caring attitude by implementing an employee assistance programme, they can continue to seek the following ideal:

In order that people may be happy in their work, these three things are needed:

– They must be fit for it,
– they must not do too much of it, and
– they must have a sense of success in it.
   (John Ruskin, 1851.)

7

Succession Management

by Peter Wallum

There has been a wholly justified resurgence of interest in succession planning in recent years. Organisations have realised that they need to make the best use of their internal human resources and that talented individuals wish to be involved in their own career planning. Constant change means that skills can rapidly become redundant and that if planned development of individuals does not take place both they and their employers will suffer. These activities are a central plank of effective performance management.

Succession Planning

Succession planning is the business of identifying particular individuals as possible successors for specific posts and suitable posts for particular individuals. Unfortunately, many firms believe that this is a largely mechanistic process and that acquiring clever off-the-shelf computer software solves the problem. Nothing could be further from the truth. What computers can do is emulate procedures and organise data to allow rapid and up-to-date interrogation and analysis. If the principles behind succession planning are faulty or the data inserted into a computer succession planning system poor, then the outcomes will be disappointing. The chore of keeping systems fed with information becomes increasingly unjustified and eventually succession planning systems fall into disrepute. Later in this chapter I describe the successful customisation of a succession planning system to meet the specific needs of a leading software house.

Succession Management

The good news is that many progressive organisations are adopting a broader, more strategic, view of what might, more correctly, be called succession management. This encompasses all activities aimed at ensuring a suitable supply of successors for senior or key posts and, in this sense, subsumes traditional succession planning within it. Effective succession management is a key element of good performance management.

What are the activities which form the core of succession management?

- Analysis of the demand for managers and professionals by level, function, skill
- Audit of existing executives and projection of likely future supply from internal and external sources
- Planning individual career paths based on objective estimates of future needs and drawing on reliable appraisals and assessments of potential
- Career counselling undertaken in the context of a realistic understanding of the future needs of the firm as well as those of the individual
- Accelerated promotion schemes with development targeted against the future needs of the business
- Performance-related training and development to prepare individuals for future roles as well as their current responsibilities
- Planned recruitment not only to fill short-term vacancies but also to provide people for development to meet future needs
- The actual processes by which jobs are filled: recruitment procedures, internal appointment procedures, methods of assessment, internal search mechanism and, often, use of computer-based information systems.

Analysis of Demand

The first element is the planning of demand for management and professional staff. In a larger firm, this will be a headcount plan detailing future levels of management for various functions within operating divisions and the skills and competences likely to be required by the job holders. While this kind of planning exercise can be exceedingly helpful there will always be an element of doubt about forecasts. Sophisticated planners are now also attempting to define the changes in corporate culture required for the future. Our work at Strategic People has developed methologies for assessing the potential 'cultural fit' of candidates against future business scenarios. Indeed, the vagaries of forecasting are probably best managed through the concept of scenario planning. Perhaps three forecasts of demand might be prepared, based on three possible business situations: optimistic, pessimistic and realistic. For larger organisations, working to long-time scales, projections might encompass 20-year plans for, say, graduate recruitment. However, for most organisations a three-year demand forecast represents sufficient challenge in today's fast-changing climate.

Audit of Supply

An audit of existing managers or staff with management potential is crucial to succession management. Techniques exist for making projections about which staff might reasonably be expected to remain at future dates as the internal supply of talent against future demand. The planned development of this cadre and the recruitment and development of additional resources are the positive actions which can ensure that the needs of the business are met and reduce the likelihood of executive redundancy.

Effective Appraisal

One of the more disturbing observations when conducting practical succession planning in real organisations is the way in which appraisal ratings do not seem to correlate with assessments of potential to fill top jobs. It seems that 'when the chips are down' in terms of nominating people for possible appointments, quite different judgements are frequently made from those arising from face-to-face appraisal discussions. The other key point is that it is always important to note whose view is being recorded. Different people rate in different ways (as discussed in Chapter 4) and this is a fact of life that one cannot ignore. Despite these comments, however, the information arising from the appraisal process is a key element in succession management and, as other chapters have shown, can be improved through training.

Planning Career Paths

In what remains a seller's market for individuals of real ability, the potentially highly mobile executive will want to have a clearer idea of the progression and variety of experience that an employer can offer. Specifically, he or she will wish to be involved in the succession planning process itself. This involvement could range from self-appraisal, as part of an open performance appraisal process, to a career development system which fully incorporates individual aspirations. For example, the organisation might ask individuals to prioritise their preference for geographical location, function or subsidiary. With dual career families and increasing concern about quality of life, this is an area of growing importance in succession management.

While it may be reassuring to know that top management undertakes systematic succession planning, modern managers will also wish to know what the company thinks of their performance and what development, including training, can help both improve current performance and prepare for promotion or an interesting sideways move. Incidentally, with organisations reducing levels of management, such sideways moves are increasing and have become as much of a focus for succession planning as promotions.

Successful managers have always been characterised by a clear view of where they want to go. Organisations need to help these highly motivated people early in their career to get the breadth of experience and quality of training which will prepare them for early responsibility. The aim of succession management will increasingly be to move high-potential employees just *before* they are really ready.

Accelerated Promotion Schemes

Larger organisations have traditionally held the belief that if sufficient high-quality graduates are recruited year by year then good managers will 'emerge' over time. This has undoubtedly been something of a wasteful process in terms both of overhead costs and the resultant under-utilisation and personal frustration of talented individuals. The increasingly competitive economy will drive this practice out of all but the most complacent organisations. Some processes for identifying and nurturing talent, graduate or otherwise, are vital since it is known that fast-track individuals have only a limited time to gain crucial experience.

The identification of 'fast-trackers' is increasingly being supported by the use of assessment or development centres (see also Chapters 3 and 4). Employees spend time undertaking aptitude tests and personality questionnaires, and participate in highly structured exercises, such as dealing with a hypothetical management in-tray. They will also participate in observed group discussions and, sometimes, outdoor activities of the War Office

Selection Board type. From a succession management point of view it is useful to capture the information from these events for inclusion in the succession plan. However, care needs to be taken, since people develop and change. Historical assessment information might, for example, show 'poor' leadership skills for someone who through training and experience has become an 'average' performer in this area. Personality questionnaires may reflect someone's state under a particular set of circumstances at a particular point in their lives.

Accelerated promotion schemes usually expose the chosen people to management training at an early stage. Thought also needs to be given to ensuring solid functional experience and exposure to key development positions. For example, in one leading transport organisation senior management have typically worked as managers of an overseas branch on their rise to the top. Product management is the key development job in many marketing-led organisations. Typically these jobs involve unusually high autonomy, substantial people management and high personal exposure to senior managers.

Career Counselling

One of the major advantages of undertaking succession planning is that those charged with counselling employees have an objective view about the future possibilities in the organisation. It is really quite remarkable that in the past firms have been quite happy to tell people that they have the potential to reach senior management or director-level positions without firm knowledge of whether vacancies might actually be available when the time comes. This was perhaps part of a quiet conspiracy exercised by some employers to keep people sharp by fostering competition for promotions that realistic assessment shows cannot exist! Security is knowing where you stand and, increasingly, better employers are seeking to be realistic when counselling employees.

With advances in information technology it will soon be possible for individuals to interact with computers which will help them assess opportunities for themselves. One leading IT firm has developed this concept to the extent that employees can call up non-sensitive information about themselves and compare their profile with that prepared for the various jobs available within the organisation. After reviewing the fit, employees can ask to be considered for such roles as they arise.

Training and Development

Even with the best made career plans, excellent counselling and the most accurate assessment of competences required for the future, individuals will achieve their potential only if they receive timely training and development. The succession management process needs also to recognise the key role of mentors in developing their protegés. (Mentoring is a relationship in which the mentor is responsible for overseeing the career and development of another person, the protegé, outside the normal line manager/subordinate relationship.)

When top managers are asked how they achieved their success, they frequently refer to key people either for whom they have worked or to whom they have turned for advice and counsel in a mentoring relationship. Within an organisation the same names frequently crop up as major influences on the development of top people. This is no coincidence. As with much of the art of performance management, the human factor reappears. There are some people who seem to have the knack of identifying, nurturing and even sponsoring talent within an organisation. The influence of these people can be much greater than formal training events, and the inspired succession manager will know how and when to expose highfliers to these natural people-developers.

The mentor and/or line manager are also important conveyors of the organisation's values and ethics. One of the difficulties in succession management is that while it is relatively easy to quantify skills and competences, a major determinant of managerial success is the effective communication of a clear vision to create a strong (appropriate) culture and set of ethics for the organisation.

Recruitment Plans

Recruitment is a much underrated activity within the personnel function, yet it is the very basis of sound performance management. Unless the raw material is sound, efforts on training and development are largely wasted. The type of people who are invited to join an organisation will also be a major determinant of the values of that organisation and its resultant culture.

Organisations of the future are likely to have a core of managers who will buy in expertise to solve problems and handle major projects. Succession management will focus on these core people. They will be the inspirational leaders of multi-disciplinary teams, the sensitive selectors and developers of people. They will also need to understand the organisation, its market and its production processes. The key task of succession management is to identify and develop these strategic people who could emerge from any discipline within the company. Whereas British industry has traditionally appointed its top ranks from the accountancy profession, the broad management skills will be as likely to come from talented individuals with a background in marketing, operations or human resource management.[1]

Succession plans will indicate where gaps in future management structures are likely to occur and will naturally lead to ways of planning the future recruitment of people by level, location and function. The aim will be to provide sufficient 'cover' in the longer term for senior posts but not to have a surplus of frustrated talent with artificial ceilings on what they are able to contribute in the organisation.

Processes for Filling Jobs

Some organisations have totally open selection procedures. It is not unknown in the public sector for quite junior or otherwise inappropriate internal candidates to offer themselves for consideration for advertised senior positions. While it is healthy for vacancies to be publicised, performance at an internal selection 'board' cannot replace the organisation's cumulative view of performance and potential built up over a period of years (manager's appraisals, development workshops and so on). Equally, appointments are sometimes made to develop an individual who may not be the best person for the immediate job but will benefit the organisation most in the longer term.

Succession management is viewed by some people as secretive or manipulative. One of the advantages of the growing use of computers in succession planning is that information in it is largely available to individuals under the Data Protection Act (see paragraph below under this heading).

Managers have been forming views on people and planning their promotion and development ever since three or more were gathered together. At least under modern performance management techniques the outcomes are shared with colleagues and views about individuals are tested in discussion and debate. Patronage of the traditional sort was often a question of personality or even social background, determined by secretive top managers who felt little need to justify or even explain their succession decisions.

Succession Management as Part of the Performance Management Process

Any planning activity will be worthwhile only if it is incorporated in the continuing management processes of an organisation. Otherwise it is a one-off exercise which, although extremely useful, will rapidly become out of date and therefore irrelevant. Succession planning used to be seen as a once-a-year exercise. Usually it was driven by top management who felt that in order to meet their responsibilities to shareholders they needed at least to have thought about succession cover for top-level jobs. Unfortunately the results of these exercises were often beautifully prepared but rapidly forgotten after the company's AGM. The fact that succession plans were prepared in this way meant that when someone fell under the proverbial 'red bus', the succession plans were found to be out of date and unhelpful.

Computers allow for the maintenance of up-to-date succession plans without the chore of having to retype the whole exercise. When someone leaves it is straightforward to pick up the consequences for succession planning. Computers are also ideal for internal search enquiries to list, for example, all staff with certain experience, qualifications, languages and managerial competencies. Regular reports on the 'state of the nation' can literally be produced at the touch of a button. The use of PC-based computer software for succession management has transformed this, like so many other, areas of management.

A succession plan should be much more than an organisation chart showing who will succeed whom. It should first of all set the business scene against which future succession will take place. It should indicate the likely shape and size of the organisation and the content of future management jobs. A succession plan should not be rigid and fixed at a point in time. It should be a flexible framework which can be adjusted to cope with changes in business plans, unexpected resignations or the emergence of new talent by recruitment or, for example, from an acquisition.

In the Strategic People approach to developing customized computer software to support succession management processes the following simple business logic is used:

- What are the business objectives?
- What skills and competences do we need to achieve them?
- What skills do our professional and managerial staff possess?
- How do we bridge this gap in the future?

While the logic is simple the process of converting business plans into human resource needs is far from simple. Some analysis can be done by examining past trends, calculating possible management ratios, making deductions from inter-firm comparisons and so on. However, at the end of the day, line management has to form a view about the numbers, levels and competences of professional and managerial staff required to implement business plans.

For this reason we often find ourselves interviewing heads of divisions or departments and talking through the future staffing needs of the unit and the implications for succession and career planning. Involvement in these processes rapidly makes it clear that line managers increasingly work from the logic of: What skills do I have in my control or can I access through internal or external recruitment to meet the business plan? The implications of this logic can be quite devastating.

One retail organisation walked away from a major acquisition because the succession planning exercise had brought into sharp relief the shortage of cover for the existing management structure. One of the rationales of the proposed acquisition had been that the management of the target company was poor and would be replaced by the acquiring firm. While this seemed true on the face of it, there simply was not enough in-depth management talent to control and lead both businesses effectively.

Another organisation was pressed by head office to diversify into attractive developing areas of business. Competitors were seen to be earning substantial returns from these activities. Succession planning helped them to work through the needs for professional and managerial staff to develop the new opportunities. Without a substantial and expensive recruitment drive it was clear that the firm did not have the resources to enter the new areas of business. Substantial recruitment of outsiders would dilute the strong culture of this organisation to an unacceptable degree. Diversification was thus limited to areas where there was an adequate supply of internal potential to be diverted into new activities without putting existing successful business at risk.

The usefulness of undertaking a succession planning exercise at times of significant potential change is increasingly being recognised. However, many companies find it difficult to sustain interest in succession management on a continuous basis. One aspect of performance management which has generally become an accepted annual – or even more frequent – activity is appraisal (see Chapter 4) or the career review discussion. If succession planning can be associated with the annual appraisal process then it can at least ensure that it is given serious detailed attention at the time of the year when management is more predisposed to longer-term thinking. Another potential anchor point is, of course, the preparation of the annual business plan or budget. Figure 7.1 illustrates how succession planning can become part of the annual cycle of performance management activity.

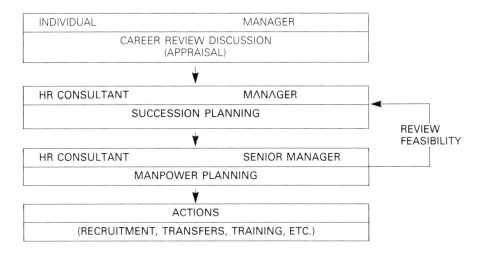

Figure 7.1 The Annual Cycle of Performance Management

The HR consultant can be internal or external, but the process of review by the senior manager is crucial, not just to verify judgements about people and to help ensure consistency in appraisal but also to incorporate informed judgement about future headcount needs. It is a unique element of this approach that it tries to ensure the validity of succession plans against the future people needs of the business, something that is rather confusingly called manpower planning

The Benefits of Succession Management

Serious succession planning is time-consuming, resource-hungry and a high-profile activity involving line management. Given the difficulty in business planning in a fast-changing world, what are the potential benefits of succession planning? The textbooks list the following potential benefits:[2]

- Emergency cover (although this does not require complex succession planning)
- Advance job filling – this really amounts to making appointments ahead of requirement and is not how most organisations fill vacancies
- Candidate listing – this seems to be the major objective of short-term succession planning for senior posts and has a number of purposes: reassuring top management, broadening fields of candidates, speeding up appointments and aiding career counselling
- Planned development – moving people with potential through the organisation in a planned way to offer broadening experiences, exposure to a range of top managers and hence their commitment to later promotions
- Improved career counselling – the use of objective succession information where career counselling is offered can make the process more relevant to the organisation's future needs
- Planned training and development – the selection of training and development opportunities with succession in mind as opposed to the needs of the current job.

Spin-off benefits are identified as: a higher profile for human resource professionals; greater understanding of the business for line managers involved in the process; the reinforcement of corporate culture by discussing people across the whole of the business; commitment to corporate as opposed to local needs; and a better quality of debate on resourcing issues.

The Problems

It would be irresponsible not to mention the considerable potential problems associated with succession planning. A major difficulty is the volatility of organisations. For instance, our succession management work with one organisation over the period of a year saw no fewer than three re-organisations. Yet even if structures remain the same, the skill and competences required do not.

People are changing employers more frequently and unpredictably. Attrition rates are useful in making overall judgements about numbers of people likely to remain at a point of time in the future, but it is very difficult to predict resignation or dismissal on an individual basis. More open job-filling processes allow people to decide for themselves which jobs to apply for. If appointment depends on being the best person at interview from those who have applied internally, this can confound succession plans.

Divisions now have greater autonomy, so succession planning may come under the control of head offices only for top jobs. Conversely, divisions can succession plan to only a certain level because of head office involvement in senior appointments.

Succession planning is only as good as the information used to prepare the plan. The easy acceptance of poor information, reflecting either the personal political agendas of top managers or inadequate personnel assessment techniques, can lead to the development of unreliable plans.

Finally, there is an inherent conflict between filling jobs with the best available candidate at a point in time and using appointments as development opportunities for fast-trackers.

Case Study: Thorn EMI Software

This case study is included to give a practical example of succession planning within the performance management framework. It draws from a joint paper the author presented to the IPM/IMS Computers in Personnel Conference 1990 with Mike Smith, the Chairman and Chief Executive of Thorn EMI Software[3] (now, since a management buy-out, Data Sciences).

Background

Mike Smith was formerly Group Chief Executive of the CAP Group plc and architect of its growth and public flotation prior to the eventual merger with the French software house, SEMA. His new appointment saw the merger of three existing Thorn EMI businesses into a new strategic business committed to becoming one of the world's top 10 companies in the computer services industry. The businesses were Software Sciences, an innovator in major software systems development, integration and project management; TECS, which distributes packaged software and management support systems; and Datasolve, a computer services operation.

These businesses had been run, in Mike Smith's words, as a 'sort of loose conglomerate with quite different management styles, reward packages and response lines, but sharing a market'. The management brief was to take these three established businesses and restructure and realign them as a new market-facing division with one mission – to become the leading provider of systems integration and facilities management services in Europe.

Smith was new to all three companies and, what was more, there was no one person in the new division who had a grasp of senior management resources other than in their own company. What was needed was a straightforward way of making all the senior management talent visible. There were a variety of personnel database systems in use within the three companies – and not a hope of making them compatible! In any case, the appraisal methodology and grading systems used by each business were quite different.

Mike Smith knew there were probably crucial gaps in the division's skill base but could not identify where they were or if they could be filled from existing resources within the organisation. Beyond these urgent problems, there was a need for a proper basis for planning management resources, recruitment and development, in the long term.

Developing a Management Succession System

The brief for the succession planning system was that it would be accepted as beneficial by all parties and so a customised system was preferred which drew on our experience in succession management and used an ingenious set of software modules which could be built to reflect Thorn EMI Software's unique needs.

The computer software system was developed within a month and line managers were interviewed to gather information on the entire management team to drive the system. Mike Smith describes the reaction: 'It is fair to say the reaction to the concept of succession planning ranged from the enthusiastic to the downright sceptical. However, everyone who has used the system so far has been won over, particularly by the natural way it disciplines one's thinking in assessing people and jobs and thereby imposes a consistency of approach without forcing it.'

The consultancy assignment included general advice on the process of succession planning and training the three company personnel managers and Group Human Resources Director to operate the system. Three sub-systems were installed which could be consolidated for the group as a whole to form a 'master' system which also included head office senior staff.

The system was designed to be easily kept up-to-date so that succession planning could become a dynamic part of the business. Different assumptions can be made about future headcount, management structures and so on which are then worked through the system to result in revised succession plans. This facilitates the link between planning the headcount needs of the business and individual career planning.

The Strategic People System is structured to hold individual skills and performance data, training records, development needs and detailed plans for an individual's possible job moves. Within this framework, the entry screens and the plans, analyses and printed reports can be tailored to allow the user, through a series of menu selections, to explore various strategies.

Potential Use of Succession Planning Information

This succession planning system differs from personnel or training databases in that it is a proactive planning tool. It does not attempt to store *all* the data relating to an individual – only that required for a range of powerful enquiries designed to enable organisations to make the fullest use of their key human resources. The system integrates existing appraisal, assessment, development and skills/competence data.

Through the computer, human resource professionals have, on tap, a live source of up-to-date information which can be searched for various purposes, such as identifying internal candidates with required skills, competence and experience profiles. Figure 7.2 illustrates the potential uses of information derived from the succession planning system.

Typical information stored for individuals includes:

- basic personal details
- current job
- functional experience
- performance assessment from appraisals or development centres
- major project experience
- training completed
- qualifications
- language capability
- training and development needs
- succession plan.

The data screens for Thorn EMI Software were designed around the structured interviews with line managers, a portable computer was used at the interviews and print-outs of the results could be prepared instantly for checking and approval. A major need was to ensure the sensible structuring of data. In an ideal world, for example, there would be master lists of job functions

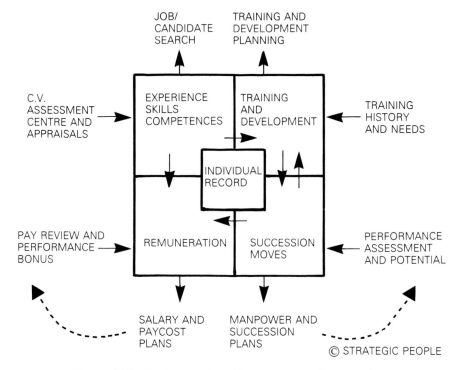

Figure 7.2: Orchestrating Management Succession

and competencies from which to 'mix and match'. However, we are nowhere near that yet; the activities of different organisations encompass quite different functional activities and competencies.

At Thorn EMI Software there were all the usual business activities – finance, personnel, marketing – but also fairly specific and important functions such as project management and facilities management. Working with company management we structured these functions with sub-functions to allow for systematic enquiries.

For example, finance might be coded as follows:

5.0 Finance
    5.1 treasury
    5.2 financial accounting
    5.3 management accounting
    5.4 tax
    5.5 planning and control.

This structure allows the computer software to search either at sub-function level, e.g. 5.4 tax, or at the general level of 5.0 Finance. Within each functional area, various levels of experience are defined in the system, together with the dates involved. The system is often used to produce current career histories. Another spin-off benefit of succession planning systems is the automatic production of up-to-date organisation charts and career histories, thus eliminating a tedious typing chore.

Another feature of the succession planning system is that it incorporates and analyses data on competences and skills, which often have to be developed with company managers. A key point is that competences or skills are always carefully researched and accurately described. Rating scales are also rigorously defined to ensure consistency of assessment and recording.

System Outputs

Various analyses and reports could be derived from the system developed for use at Thorn EMI Software. The various users of the system and the outputs they required are listed below:

Personnel Managers
- resourcing of internal vacancies
- succession planning (in consultation with other units)
- local manpower planning/headcount 'budgeting'
- project staffing
- tracking of performance-improvement actions
- rapid response to general enquiries, e.g. for specific languages.

Training Managers
- training needs analysis
- forecast of training demand with priority areas
- tracking of broader development plans
- assessing effectiveness of training in relation to performance.

Personnel Director
- corporate succession and manpower planning
- fast-track development
- senior internal resourcing
- management audit.

Chief Executive
- human resource data instantly available for input to Board decision-making and organisational reviews

- top-level internal resourcing
- measure of effectiveness of HR policies and programmes
- additional information to review corporate strategy, e.g. HR capability for entering new markets or making acquisitions.

Data Protection

An obvious concern to anyone introducing a computerised succession planning system is the degree of openness to staff and questions relating to the Data Protection Act. The various organisations that have introduced systems have registered them under the provisions of the Act and have been quite content to show individuals personal data relating to themselves. Questions of 'intention' do not, however, need to be open to employees, especially as they will also relate to other people's succession moves. This effectively excludes the specific planned succession from disclosure provision.

Conclusions

Succession management is a term used to describe the various activities aimed at ensuring a suitable supply of successors to senior or key posts. Succession management is one of the main strategic activities of the personnel function – it is business-driven and concerned with the longer-term success of the organisation. Succession planning is just part of the succession management process and is about identifying particular individuals as possible successors for specific posts and suitable posts for specific individuals.

This chapter has been realistic about the difficulties of succession management in a today's fast-changing business environment. The fact that all strategic planning is difficult and subject to error does not invalidate the value of undertaking it. Organisations can improve the quality of their succession planning by auditing the information about people and future jobs that are central to their plans. They can also improve plans by fully involving line management in the process and effectively communicating the outcomes. A clear trend for the future is that individuals will wish their career expectations and wider aspirations to be taken more fully into account than hitherto.

Computer technology has transformed the possibilities for performance management. The Strategic People System described above and other similar systems can run on widely used portable or standard PCs and be networked if desired. Only a few years ago it would have required a mainframe, with all the associated complications. The case study illustrates the degree of sophistication that leading firms are now adopting in the management of their principal resource – their strategic people.

8

The Feedback Loop

by Pamela Pocock

In reality, there is a sense in which no performance management cycle is ever complete. The process is both evolutionary and iterative, as has been pointed out by many of the authors in this book. The constituent parts of a performance management system should never be viewed in isolation and the outcomes should be fed back to those planning the future of the business. Only if the loop is closed in this way can an organisation's human resource strategy become an integral part of the business strategy and be respected as such by line managers.

Predictability, as the management gurus tell us, is a thing of the past. Nowadays we are all encouraged to be responsive to the changes in the business environment around us and to the evolving needs of our customers. However, as Tom Peters points out in *Thriving on Chaos*, this responsiveness is unlikely to be spearheaded by the strategic planners in their ivory tower – or head office:

> The new strategic plan, and planning process, must necessarily be 'bottom-up'. Assessing the ability (and necessary skills) to execute – to be responsive, flexible, attentive to customers – starts on the front line. Obviously, as the process moves forward, it will involve debate among senior officers, and compromise. But it should never lose touch with or sight of the front line, where execution takes place.

Part of this bottom-up process will, of course, be the feedback from the performance management process. In ICL, we are told, consolidation of all the individual outputs from these plans forms the basis for a review of the total organisational capability of each part of the company – in terms of succession, career development, training and level of skills and knowledge. This information is then formally linked to the business review.

An iterative approach of this kind is necessary if we are to develop learning organisations which maximise the potential of all those who work within them. Such an argument would not be at all unfamiliar to a marketing executive who relies on the market research information which he or she regularly receives to plan campaigns and launch new products. It seems strange that the majority of organisations are reluctant to build up the same kind of data on the people that it employs.

If we start by examining the foundation of any performance management system – objective setting and performance measurement – one of the first lessons to be learnt is that objectives should not be set in tablets of stone. Organisations which are responsive to the needs of their staff as well as to those of their customers will ensure that there is a regular review built in to the process, probably on a quarterly basis. Indeed, there are those who feel that this is not sufficiently frequent and that only a continuous process can reflect the fluid nature of the world around us.

Individual objectives and targets are often developed from the corporate or business objectives which are cascaded down through the organisation. Building on Tom Peters' argument, we can see that continual review of individual objectives can provide an organisation with its antennae in the marketplace. Those in the front line, particularly in sales-driven organisations, will be the first to know when the corporate objectives are no longer sensible. They may have heard rumours of a new product launch from a competitor, or felt the first chill winds of a recession. Alternatively, they may become aware of a new market niche or product opportunity, simply by listening to the needs of their customers. The responsive organisation will take this information on board as part of its two-way communication and will use it to set the course for the future. Unfortunately, we hear all too often stories of people who have left organisations and set up in business on their own just because their former employer was unwilling to listen to and act upon their ideas.

Performance management, therefore, is not simply for the benefit of the organisation. It should be designed positively to encourage people to reach their full potential. Appraisal, coaching and counselling are part of that process and managers' responsibilities to staff in these areas are clearly outlined in earlier chapters in this book.

In terms of the organisation, considerable information is generated during the formal appraisal which should be captured and fed back into other parts of the performance management system.

Appraisal data is commonly one source of information for succession management in any organisation. However, as has been pointed out in the chapter on that subject, the data produced from appraisal ratings is not always in accord with that which would be advanced by a line manager on a confidential basis. Where this happens, there is a definite break in the performance management system which will need attention. There is also a distinct education and training need.

Education is required to help managers understand how data on employees is consolidated within a firm, and how it can be used as part of the strategic planning process. It is also important for them to realise the consequences for the individuals who have not been given the information that will help them to improve their performance. All too frequently personnel departments are faced with an instruction to fire someone on the basis of poor performance whose appraisal ratings have consistently been above average!

If there is a gap between the formal appraisal ratings and managers' confidential ranking of subordinates, then there is obviously a skills training need. However, there may also be a cultural issue, since some organisations do not always encourage mature and supportive attitudes among their employees – perhaps because it is more important to be politically astute. Bad news is not readily shared and there is a tendency to 'shoot the messenger'. To be successful, performance management systems need to be built in to a culture where honesty is valued and where openness leads to greater understanding and trust.

Other outputs from the appraisal process which should be fed back to the business-unit level include training needs and career development plans. It may well be that a review of the training and development needs flagged up by individuals in the unit will reveal a generic demand for training (for example, financial awareness in a newly privatised organisation). Career development outcomes from appraisal must be fed back into a central process. This is likely to be some form of succession or career management system.

Interestingly, training programmes are also an integral part of the feedback loop. It is most important that those who are involved as tutors and facilitators are aware of the organisational issues being raised by course participants. For example, we recently ran an appraisal training scheme for a financial services company. As a result of this work it became clear that objective setting in the firm was really synonymous with target setting and that the whole process was task-focused. This knowledge was strategically important since the organisation was entering a stage in its growth where developmental objectives would become more important if it was to retain its impressive track record. In this instance, the feedback loop was completed by the trainers and the human resource specialist working together to impart this information to the Board of Directors.

This is an example of a learning organisation at work and clearly demonstrates that the learning cycle outlined by Alan Mumford in Chapter 3 does not apply simply to individuals. There is also, of course, a relationship between skills-based training and the manager's duty to coach and to counsel. On the basis that 'learning by doing' is extremely powerful, the onus is on every manager to ensure that his or her staff have the opportunity to implement their newly acquired skills on the job.

But what will ensure that managers behave in the way that has been suggested? Generally speaking, the most powerful inducement is the reward structure, which is where performance-related pay is linked to and can influence many parts of the performance management system. For example, if the senior managers in an organisation felt that investment in training and development was not bringing a commensurate improvement in performance, they might decide that improved coaching skills were the answer. This decision would then have to be translated into each person's individual objectives. Performance would then be measured against these objectives and pay based on that assessment. The most likely outcome would surely be an improvement in coaching skills throughout the organisation.

It is links such as these that show the interdependence of all parts of a performance management system. They also demonstrate the need to constantly review the process. To date many organisations' experience of performance-related pay, for example, has been that the structure that they so willingly embraced at the start of the year is not sufficiently flexible to cope with the changes that emerge subsequently. The recession in 1991 is a case in point where there has been a need to re-assess objectives and hence the basis for the performance element of pay. Such a re-assessment of objectives is not, of course, to be confused with the oft-quoted management ploy of moving the goalposts!

One of the more formal links in the performance management feedback process must be a central career management system. For example, performance ratings and career development outcomes from appraisal would both be fed back into a central process. Nowadays such systems are likely to be computer-based and so can accommodate changes in information rapidly. This speed is of the essence in a fast-changing business environment where up-to-date human resource information can be at the heart of a corporate decision to enter a new market or make an acquisition.

In the same way, changes in strategic direction or business plans must be taken into account by the career management system; indeed, such systems may well have a capacity for scenario-based planning. Once again there are benefits here for the individual as well as the organisation. In the past, some managers have been prepared to tell people that they could be promoted to a senior level within the organisation without being aware whether such opportunities will exist in the future or not. In more recent times, particularly with the reduction in levels of management in organisations, it has become imperative to deal honestly with people so they have a clear view of the opportunities which are open to them and can make their choices on that basis.

So we can see that there are interrelationships between all the elements of the performance management process and that each can produce information which needs to be fed directly back into future business plans. But what is the role of the human resource specialist in all this? In my opinion, the most significant roles must be those of catalyst and facilitator: a catalyst in terms of gaining the commitment of those at the top and in actually defining the process; and a facilitator in terms of providing the appropriate training and in communicating the benefits to every employee of the organisation.

On top of this, the most influential role that a human resource director can play will be to capture all the outcomes from the performance management process and ensure that they are acted upon in planning the future of the business. Only then will the function become truly strategic.

References

Introduction
1 T. Peters, *Thriving on Chaos*, Pan/Macmillan, 1989.
2 C. Handy, *The Age of Unreason*, Business Books, 1989.
3 R. Townsend, *Up the Organisation*, Michael Joseph, 1970.

Chapter 3: Performance-related Skills Training
1 R. Boyatzis, *The Competent Manager*, Wiley, 1982.
2 P. Honey and A. Mumford, *Manual of Learning Styles*, Peter Honey, 1986.
3 A. Mumford, *Developing Top Managers*, Gower, 1988.
4 A. Mumford, *Management Development: Strategies for Action*, IPM, 1989.
5 M. Pedler, J. Burgoyne and T. Boydell, *Self Development for Managers*, McGraw-Hill, 1986.
6 P. Honey and A. Mumford, *Manual of Learning Opportunities*, Peter Honey, 1989.

Chapter 4: Appraisal
1 G. Randell, P. Packard and J. Slater, *Staff Appraisal*, IPM, 1972, 1984.
2 P. Long, *Performance Appraisal Revisited*, IPM, 1986.

Chapter 5: Performance-related Pay
1 Survey published in *Personnel Today*, November 1990.
2 Unpublished pilot study of Performance Management in High Peforming Companies, Institute of Personnel Management, 1990.
3 and 4 Hay Management Consultants, 1989.
5 V. Wright, 'Profit Sharing and Profit Related Pay', *Personnel Management*, November 1986.
6 J. A. Fossum and M. K. Fitch, 'The Effects of Individual and Contextual Attributes on the Sizes of Recommended Salary Increases', *Personnel Psychology*, Autumn 1985.
7 See reference 3 above.
8 N. Kinnie and D. Lowe, 'Performance Related Pay on the Shop Floor', *Personnel Management*, November 1990.
9 Pilot Study of Performance Management In High Performing Companies, Institute of Personnel Management, 1990.
10 F. F. Reichheld and W. Earl Sasser Jr, 'Zero Defections: Quality Comes to Services', *Harvard Business Review*, September/October 1990.

11 Good examples include M. Armstrong and H. Murlis, *Reward Management* (Kogan Page/IPM, 1991); R. Greenhill, *Performance Related Pay* (Director Books, 1988); and the Incomes Data Services – Top Pay Unit Research File 9 on *Paying For Performance* (IDS, July 1988).

Chapter 6: Counselling and Coaching
1 Industrial Society, *Blueprint for Success: A Report on Involving Employees in Britain*, 1989.
2 T. Allison, C. L. Cooper and P. Reynolds (1989), 'Stress Counselling in the Workplace – The Post Office Experience', *Psychologist*, September 1989.
3 M. Devine, 'The listening managers', *Sunday Times*, 12 February 1989.
4 P. Honeyborne, National Personnel Manager, ITT World Directories (UK) Ltd., speaking at the European EAP Conference, London, 26 April 1991.
5 G. Egan, speaking at the ICAS London Workshop, July 1990.
6 Distributive Industries Training Board, *Coach to Succeed*.
7 BBC2 television programme, Business Matters series, *Workers in Mind*, May 1990.
8 C. R. Rogers, *Client-Centered Therapy*, Houghton Mifflin, Boston, 1951.
9 G. Egan, *The Skilled Helper*, Brooke Cole, Monterey, 1986.
10 M. Reddy, *The Manager's Guide to Counselling at Work*, British Psychological Society/Methuen, London, 1987.
11 D. Geldard, *Basic Personal Counselling*, Prentice Hall, Australia, 1989.
12 S. Crown and A. H. Crisp *Manual of the Crown Crisp Experiential Index*, Hodder and Stoughton Educational, 1979.
13 P. Warr, J. Cook and T. Wall, 'Scales for the Measurement of Some Work Attitudes and Aspects of Psychological Wellbeing', *Journal of Occupational Psychology*, Vol. 52, 1979.
14 Dr P. Saville, *Contemporary Trends in Assessment*, SHL Conference, September 1990.
15 G. Sadri, C. L. Cooper and T. Allison, 'A Post Office Initiative to Stamp Out Stress', *Personnel Management*, August 1989.
16 Health and Safety Executive, *Mental Health at Work*, HMSO, London, 1988.
17 V. Mosher, EAPA International Representative, speaking at the European EAP Conference, London, 27 April 1991.
18 L. Hoskinson and M. Reddy, *Counselling Services in UK Organisations*, ICAS, 1989.
Other useful books are

E. J. Singer, *Effective Management Coaching* (IPM, 1987); J. Hunt, *Managing People at Work* (IPM/McGraw-Hill, 1986); W. Halston, 'Teaching Supervisors to Coach', *Personnel Management*, March 1990; and M. Megranahan, *Counselling: A Practical Guide for Employers* (IPM, 1989).

Chapter 7: Succession Management
1 P. Wallum, 'Mastering Motivation', in *The Complete Guide to Modern Management 1991–92*, edited by Robert Heller (Mercury Books, 1990).
2 .W. Hirsh, *Succession Planning: Current Practice and Future Issues*, Report No 184, Institute of Manpower Studies, 1990.
3 M. Smith and P. Wallum, *Succession Planning in Business Strategy: Orchestrating Management Succession*, 1990.